Introduction

The answers which follow have been compiled witl
really want to learn Latin Book III with an easy to us
their work. The answers are in no way meant to b
course be allowed, in particular with regard to word c
possible, suggested translations are those which it is
by a student who had reached that stage in the cour.

Chapter 1

Exercise 1.1

1. *vocāns, vocantis*
2. *pugnāns, pugnantis*
3. *manēns, manentis*
4. *discēns, discentis*
5. *iēns, euntis*
6. *trahēns, trahentis*
7. *vertēns, vertentis*
8. *vincēns, vincentis*
9. *cōnficiēns, cōnficientis*
10. *lūdēns, lūdentis*

Exercise 1.2

1. He watched the ships sailing into the harbour.
2. The Gauls saw the Roman men sitting in the forum.
3. The boys captured the horse (which was) standing near the wall.
4. We were watching the Roman general leading the soldiers into battle.
5. I heard the poet singing in the garden.
6. The Trojans were not sufficiently fearful of the Greeks (who were) bearing gifts.
7. The slave saw the master going into the fields.
8. The powerful king terrified the people.
9. The ambassador was seen by the women hurrying out of the forum.
10. Why are you, standing in the garden, singing and shouting?

Exercise 1.3

1. *puerōs in agrum currentēs spectāvimus.*
2. *fīlius dōnum mātrī dedit.*
3. *sub arbore sedēns, agricola servōs spectābat.*
4. *agricola servōs sub arbore sedentēs spectābat.*
5. *imperātor mīlitēs pugnantēs laudāvit.*
6. *magister prope puerōs puellāsque sedēns librum legēbat.*
7. *nēmō nōmen puellae dormientis scit.*
8. *num servī Rōmānōs pugnantēs superābunt?*
9. *cūr fēminae puerum in hortō flentem relīquērunt?*
10. *poētamne īn forō cantantem audīvistī?*

So you really want to learn Latin...

Exercise 1.4

1. Deciding; constituent
2. Doing; agent
3. Walking; ambulance
4. Climbing; ascendency
5. Hearing; audience
6. Falling; cadence
7. Compelling; cogent
8. Believing; credence
9. Driving back; repellent
10. Waiting; expectant

Exercise 1.5

A farmer had five sons. The sons were often arguing and did not work well. Their father therefore gave a bundle of sticks to one son and asked "Can you break this bundle of sticks?" The boy could not break the bundle. Then the father gave the bundle of sticks to the second son. "Can you break this bundle of sticks?" the father asked. He could not. Soon all the boys tried to break the bundle of sticks, but in vain. Then the farmer untied the bundle and gave the sticks to his sons one at a time. The boys easily broke the sticks. Then the father laughingly said "Alone you are not strong. Together, however, you will be overcome by noone!"

Exercise 1.6

1. *agricola in agrīs labōrābat, terram parāns.*
2. *"num omnēs frātrēs" fīliō inquit "vincere potes?"*
3. *puer ad frātrēs cucurrit et gladium tenēns eōs vulnerāre cōnātus est.*
4. *pater īrātus est et fīliōs pugnantēs rapuit.*
5. *"validī estis" inquit "sed, sōlī pugnantēs, inimīcōs superāre nōn potestis."*

Exercise 1.7

1. All were rejoicing, hurrying into the forum.
2. Marcus found his sister crying under the table.
3. You want to watch the ships sailing into the harbour, don't you?
4. The leader of the army watched the soldiers pitching camp near the river.
5. Where did the citizens (who were) praising the queen come from?

Exercise 1.8

1. We were watching the Gauls who were about to attack the city.
2. The soldiers, about to fight for their fatherland, were preparing their weapons.
3. Ulysses, who was about to return home, gave thanks to the gods.
4. What kind of man laughs when he is about to kill a young man?
5. Hannibal watched the enemy who were about to pitch camp.

Exercise 1.9

1. The small boy saw the farmer who had been killed.
2. The slave who had been found was sent home as quickly as possible.
3. The girl gave the book, which she had read, to her friend.
4. We were unable to find the girl who had been left by her mother.
5. The ship which had been built in the harbour was destroyed by the storm.

So you really want to learn Latin...

Exercise 1.10
1. *equōs in agrum ambulantēs vidēmus.*
2. *equitēs oppidum oppugnātūrōs vīdērunt.*
3. *servōs captōs īn forum dūxit.*
4. *mīlitēs pugnātūrī ducibus suīs semper pārent.*
5. *dī cīvibus victīs īrāscī vidēbantur.*
6. *iuvenis dōnum pulchrum sub mēnsā relictum invēnit.*
7. *cōnsul mīlitēs īn forō cum captīvīs loquentēs spectāvit.*
8. *Rōmānī aliud bellum contrā hostēs victōs gerere poterant.*
9. *mīlitēs puellam extrā mūrōs urbis lūdentem vīdērunt.*
10. *ā mīlitibus capta scūtīs eōrum interfecta est.*

Exercise 1.11
1. Perhaps the gods will come down from the sky and save the captured women.
2. I shall not read the book which has been given to me by you.
3. We were unable to find the money which had been placed under the judge's table.
4. Carry the water to the sleeping soldiers during the night.
5. Go to Rome, Regulus, and bear peace offerings (lit. words of peace) to the Romans as quickly as possible.
6. The fortunate girls fled from the captured city.
7. Meanwhile the Carthaginians were waging war in Africa and did not free the captured legions.
8. We were able to see the children of the citizens playing in the garden.
9. The bold Gauls were unable to conquer the Romans (who were) remaining on the hill.
10. The best citizens wanted to follow the general who was hurrying across the river.

Exercise 1.12
1. *urbem oppugnātam cēpimus.*
2. *mīlitem interfectum īn silvam trāximus.*
3. *Rōmānī Gallōs superātōs ad urbem dūxērunt.*
4. *servum captum interficiam.*
5. *nōnne librum tibī datum legēs?*

Exercise 1.13
After the war the Carthaginian soldiers returned home. However the money which was owed to them was not handed over. Very angry, therefore, they advanced into the city and sought out their leader, named Hanno. They found him walking in the forum. "I can't give you your money" he said. "The Romans conquered us and we were not able to capture booty from them." Some soldiers were angry; others, however, decided to set out once more into war. Among the latter was a young man called Hannibal. He, the son of the bravest general, wanted to follow his father into Spain and gain the greatest glory.

So you really want to learn Latin...

Exercise 1.14

1. A certain general was present in Spain.
2. He wanted not only money but also very great fame.
3. Having set out into Spain he waged war for a long time.
4. He captured many buildings and always used to fight well for his fatherland.
5. The town of Saguntum was attacked by the Carthaginians.
6. "What do you think?" said a certain angry citizen "and what shall we do?"
7. We shall seek help as quickly as possible from the Romans.
8. Having spoken thus, that citizen set out silently for Rome.
9. The Roman consul listened to the Spanish ambassadors speaking in the forum.
10. Your speech has not moved us, nor do we fear enemies who are soon to die.

Exercise 1.15

imperātor Pūnicus, nōmine Hannibal, in Africā habitābat. ōlim inde profectus in Hispāniam vēnit. hīc multa bella gerēbat et multōs mīlitēs Rōmānōs capiēbat. ōlim* cum aliīs imperātōribus tacitus ambulāns hoc cōnsilium cēpit. exercitum suum in montēs dūcere cōnstituit, et inde in Ītaliam. aliī cōnsilium laudāvērunt, aliī paulum timēbant. Hannibal tamen, quī fortissimus erat, perīcula itineris nōn timēbat.

*Expressions such as "one day" or "one year" are best translated simply by *ōlim*.

Exercise 1.16

Hannibal set out from Spain with many soldiers and entered Gaul. For a long time he was able to avoid the Romans but at last he was seen by the leader of an army which was hurrying into Spain. When he learnt this Hannibal angrily asked "How many soldiers are there and where are they going? What kind of general do they have?" However before his friends were able to reply Hannibal adopted a certain plan. "We shall go into the mountains. The Romans will not follow us there. From there we shall go to Rome itself. For Rome, a city full of food and wine, will be the greatest reward for us."

Exercise 1.17

1. Hannibal's father was Hamilcar.
2. Hannibal set off for Italy with an army consisting of 38,000 foot-soldiers, 8,000 horseman and 37 elephants.
3. Before tackling the Alps Hannibal had to cross the Pyrenees.
4. Hannibal ferried his elephants across the River Rhone on rafts.
5. The Roman general Scipio failed to stop Hannibal from leading his men into the Alps.
6. The Allobroges tribe gave Hannibal and his men grief in the Alps.
7. Hannibal managed to raise the morale of his lieutenants by pointing out the plains of Italy, spread out below them like a map.
8. The Carthaginians dealt with the obstruction of a rock by heating it up, pouring vinegar over it to make it crack, and then smashing it up with pick-axes.
9. The Carthaginians finally entered Italy near the River Po.
10. They had suffered casualties of 18,000 foot-soldiers and 2,000 horsemen.

So you really want to learn Latin...

Chapter 2

Exercise 2.1
1.   After the enemy had been defeated
2.   While the father was watching
3.   After the farmer had been warned
4.   While the queen was ruling
5.   After the books had been read
6.   While noone was departing
7.   After the table had been prepared
8.   After the spears had been thrown
9.   After the ambassadors had been sent
10. After the army had set out

Exercise 2.2
1.   *rēge occīsō*
2.   *hīs factīs*
3.   *fābulā nārrātā*
4.   *iuvene sequente*
5.   *puellīs fugientibus*

Exercise 2.3
1.   After the enemy had been seen, the general led his army quickly onto the plain.
2.   After the camp had been pitched near the river, the Romans advanced towards the enemy.
3.   After the books had been read by the boys, the master told them this story.
4.   After the poet had spoken thus, the citizens were greatly afraid.
5.   Because* the words of the judge had not been understood, the slave was freed.
6.   Because* the lion had been killed by the soldier, all the citizens were rejoicing.

* Note how an ablative absolute can often be used to express a causal clause, i.e to explain *why* something happened, rather than simply *when* it happened.

Exercise 2.4
1.   *servīs monitīs dominus ad forum rediit.*
2.   *cōnsule audiente fābulam nostram populō nārrāvimus.*
3.   *mīlite occīsō pāx cum hostibus cōnfecta est.*
4.   *Rōmānīs profectīs, barbarī ad montēs fūgērunt.*
5.   *nāvibus dēlētīs omnēs nautae mortem exspectābant.*
6.   *oppidō ab hostibus oppugnātō, cīvēs fūgērunt*.

*An unfair sentence to set until the material on page 20 has been studied, but certainly one to keep them on their toes!

So you really want to learn Latin...

Exercise 2.5

1. After the temples had been built by the consul, the citizens didn't have any food.
2. They were praising the temples built by the general.
3. All the soldiers who had been captured in the battle were killed.
4. He drove the sword, which had been quickly captured, into the body of the slave.
5. After the story had been told, the master led the boy back home.
6. When the inn was suddenly seen, the farmers were happy again.
7. The Romans watched the forces who had been led across the mountains.
8. After the forces had been led across the mountains, Hannibal wanted to hurry into Italy.
9. The forces who had been led across the mountains were following Hannibal into Italy.
10. After peace had been sought from the enemy in vain, the battle raged* on the plain for three hours.

*pugnātum est : as we saw in Book II (p.74), pugnō, being an intransitive verb, cannot be used in the passive other than impersonally.

Exercise 2.6

1. Rōmānī fēminās captās interfēcērunt.
2. nautīs tabernam quaerentibus, equitēs prōgressī sunt.
3. nūllō spectante exercitus tōtus profectus est.
4. tēlīs iactīs mīlitēs fūgērunt.
5. ventō magnō ortō nautae in portū manēre cōnstituērunt.
6. agricolā vīnum parante, nōs in tabernā sedēbāmus.
7. legātōs Rōmā profectūrōs exspectābāmus.
8. hīs factīs nūntiī domum rediērunt.

Exercise 2.7

1. Nūllus = no. To nullify is to make null, i.e. to make as nothing.
2. Senātor = a senator. Senatorial means pertaining to a senator or to the senate.
3. Timor = fear. Timorous means fearful.
4. Vērus = true. Verily means truly.
5. Pūniō = I punish. Punitive means as a punishment.
6. Vetus = old. A veteran is one who has seen long service, e.g. an old soldier.
7. Vīnum = wine. Viniculture is the cultivation of vines, e.g. for wine-making.
8. Tōtus = whole. Total means whole.
9. Sōlus = alone. Sole means only, e.g. the sole survivor was a man aged forty.
10. Valē = farewell. Valedictory remarks are those made when someone is leaving.

So you really want to learn Latin...

Exercise 2.8

1. *cum nūllīs amīcīs.*
2. *num ūllī mīlitī crēdit?*
3. *puellae sōlae sedēbant.*
4. *urbem tōtam dēlēvērunt.*
5. *ūllōsne senātōrēs vīdistī?*
6. *num tōtam gentem pūniet?*
7. *habēsne ūllōs leōnēs?*
8. *fessa est neque ūllum cibum habet.*
9. *ūllōsne cīvēs occīdērunt?*
10. *Rōmam īvērunt nec tamen ūlla templa vīdērunt.*

Exercise 2.9

1. The rich citizens standing on the hill were praising the gods.
2. After our men had been overcome by the Gauls, the poor citizens sought help.
3. After the rich inhabitants had been driven to the sea, the Roman cavalry began burning the old buildings.
4. Because a great storm had arisen, the sailors sought the land as quickly as possible.
5. With the women following, the poor men returned into the fields.

Exercise 2.10

After winning these victories Hannibal wanted to hurry to Rome itself. The Carthagininans however, because the inhabitants were not helping in any way, were not able to capture the city without more forces. Therefore Hannibal, with the Romans following, led his army across Italy.

The Roman general, called Quintus Fabius Maximus, always watched the enemy but for a long time he did not fight with them. However he almost captured the enemy when he drove them between some mountains. The Romans had pitched their camp around the Carthaginians and they were unable to flee. However the Carthaginians had captured very many oxen whose horns they had decorated with lots of twigs. Setting fire to the twigs they drove these oxen towards the Romans. The Romans, some amazed, others terrified, left their battle-line and the Carthaginians escaped.

Exercise 2.11

1. The Carthaginians first defeated the Romans between the Rivers Po and Ticino.
2. The Carthaginians' second victory over the Romans was at the River Trebia.
3. Before this battle the Carthaginians covered themselves with oil to protect themselves from the cold.
4. All but one of the elephants died.
5. The Carthaginians were assisted at the Battle of Lake Trasimene by the mist rising off the lake which helped to cover their advance.
6. The Romans were further unsettled by a sudden earthquake.

So you really want to learn Latin...

7. The Roman general Quintus Fabius Maximus had to face Hannibal when the latter marched over to the Adriatic coast of Italy.
8. Fabius was at that time dictator, an office he held for six months.
9. Hannibal managed to escape through the Appenines by driving a herd of oxen, whose horns had been adorned with lighted torches, into the midst of the Roman army and throwing them into confusion.
10. Fabian tactics is the name given to the military tactic of deliberately withholding from contact with the enemy in order to wear them out. These tactics take their name from the Roman general Quintus Fabius Maximus who famously used them in the war with Hannibal.

So you really want to learn Latin...

Chapter 3

Exercise 3.1
1. *loquī vult.*
2. *fugere nōlunt.*
3. *hīc manēre mālumus.*
4. *labōrāre nōlent.*
5. *Hannibal Rōmam intrāre voluerat.*
6. *in campō pugnāre mālēbant.*
7. *nōlīte fugere ā castrīs, mīlitēs!*
8. *num ducem in montēs sequī vultis?*
9. *nōlī dūcere mīlitēs in mare!*
10. *nōlī currere ad flūmen altum, Marce!*

Exercise 3.2
1. On the next day the general drew up his forces on the plain.
2. The skill of the Carthaginian soldiers was greater than the strength of the Romans.
3. "Where are the forces of the enemy?" asked the consul.
4. The inhabitants of Italy will never yield to the enemy.
5. Fabius did not wish to lead his column across the country.
6. At last the road which led to the city was open to the Carthaginians.
7. After very many soldiers had been lost in the battle the Romans were forced to flee.
8. Scarcely one young man was found alive.
9. Do not touch the food which your mother placed on the table.
10. Do not read the books which the poet gave to me.

Exercise 3.3
multōs annōs Rōmānī bellum contrā Poenōs gerēbant nec tamen eōs vincere poterant. ōlim* autem imperātor fortissimus nōmine Hannibal, mīlitibus trāns Ītaliam ductīs, aciem prope montēs īnstrūxit. Rōmānī, castrīs positīs, aggredī parāvērunt. bōbus** tamen adiuvantibus Poenī Rōmānōs ab agmine pellere et fugere poterant. hīs audītīs cōnsulēs exercitum in bellum ipsī dūcere cōnstituērunt.

*As we saw in Exercise 1.15, expressions such as "one day" or "one year" are best translated simply by *ōlim.*

**This irregular noun is not found in full until p. 30.

Exercise 3.4
1. Will the young man run or walk?
2. Have the Romans overcome the Carthaginians or not?
3. Shall I hurry to Rome or stay here?
4. Does that farmer truly love his son or his daughter?
5. Shall we be alive or dead tomorrow?

So you really want to learn Latin...

Exercise 3.5

1. *utrum domum redīre an in urbe manēre vīs?*
2. *utrum lēgātī victōriam nūntiāvērunt annōn?*
3. *utrum bellum an pācem rēx māvult?*
4. *Rōmamne quīnque diēbus ambulāre potes annōn?*
5. *Gallīne Rōmam diē an noctū oppugnāvērunt?*

Exercise 3.6

1. *Rōmae manēbō.*
2. *Corinthī habitāre nōlunt.*
3. *nōnne Athēnīs habitāre vīs?*
4. *utrum Alexandrēae regere vult annōn?*
5. *Hannibal Carthāgine manēre nōlēbat.*
6. *omnēs agricolae rūrī labōrāre mālēbant.*
7. *domī manēte, mīlitēs!*
8. *corpus rēgis humī iacēbat.*

Exercise 3.7

1. *Proximus* = nearest. Proximity is a mesure of how near something is.
2. *Ars* = art. If someone is artistic they have skill or art.
3. *Cēdō* = I yield. If one makes a concession, one yields.
4. *Īnstruō* = I draw up. Instruction is the art of instructing or teaching. (The link with the military activity of drawing up an army in correct order for battle may appear a little tenuous.)
5. *Quantus* = how great? Quantity is a measure of the amount or size of anything.
6. *Volō* = I wish. If one does something of one's own volition, one wishes to do it.
7. *Accipiō* = I accept or receive. To accept is to receive.
8. *Aperiō* = I open. An aperture is an opening.
9. *Bōs* = an ox. Bovine means pertaining to cattle.
10. *Proximus* = nearest. Approximate means nearest or next, often used to mean very nearly correct.

Exercise 3.8

1. *agricolane cum bōbus discessit annōn?*
2. *ā nūntiō Iovis monitus rūrī manēbat.*
3. *Rōmae cīvēs vīrēs hostium timēbant.*
4. *quantum est agmen peditum Carthāgine īnstrūctum?*
5. *cōnsul librōs quōs ad eum mīsistī domī legere volēbat.*
6. *num virī quī rūrī habitant labōrantque volāre possunt?*
7. *artem pācis āmissam nēmō umquam inveniet.*
8. *nōlī amīcōs domī relinquere!*
9. *utrum Iovem an aliōs deōs adōrāre* mālēbat?*

So you really want to learn Latin...

10. *vīgintī annōs pater illĩus puerī Rōmae sōlus habitābat.*
adōrāre + acc. or *supplicō* + dat. are both preferable to *ōrō*. Sadly they don't feature in the vocabulary.

Exercise 3.9
For a long time the Romans, with Fabius as their leader, did not wish to fight with the enemy in battle. But in the next year they adopted a very bad plan. For everyone wanted to conquer the Carthaginians and indeed they had then very many forces. Therefore they decided to use not skill but force in that war. Moreover the two consuls, Lucius Aemilius Paullus and Marcus Terrentius Varro, who at that time had never fought with Hannibal, decided to lead the Roman army towards the Carthaginians.

The Carthaginians drew up their forces near a town called Cannae. In the middle of the line they placed a few foot-soldiers. Seeing this the Romans made a very great attack on the middle of the line with very many foot-soldiers. At first the enemy seemed to withdraw. However the enemy cavalry, having advanced around the wings of the Romans, drove the Roman cavalry into flight. Then they attacked the Romans in the rear.

Soon the Romans were overcome and very many were killed. After the battle the Carthaginians took the rings from the fingers of the Romans and sent them to Carthage.

Exercise 3.10
1. To wish
2. They laugh
3. They will yield
4. At home
5. In the countryside
6. To be drawn up
7. I have drawn up
8. Having been drawn up
9. To be present
10. I was absent

Exercise 3.11
1. *utrum Hannibal an Fabius imperātor sapientior erat?*
2. *cūr Rōmānī Fabiō nōn favēbant?*
3. *Rōmānīs victīs Hannibal Rōmam nōn oppugnāvit.*
4. *hic cōnsul contrā Poenōs pugnāre volēbat, ille tamen in castrīs manēre mālēbat.*
5. *proximō diē Terentius suōs in mediam aciem hostium dūxit.*
6. *exercitū superātō, multī cīvēs interfectī, cēterī captī sunt.*
7. *Aemilius Paullus fugere nōlēbat et cum mīlitibus mortuus est*
8. *cōnsul alter ē caede effūgit et Rōmam rediit.*
9. *post proelium Poenī socium, dentibus peditis Rōmānī vulnerātum, invēnit.*
10. *utrum huic fābulae crēdēmus annōn?*

So you really want to learn Latin...

Chapter 4

Exercise 4.1
1. He says that the farmers are working in the fields.
2. He says that the woman is walking in the garden.
3. He says that the soldiers are attacking the city.
4. He says that the poet loves the book.
5. I say that war is bad.

Exercise 4.2
1. *dīcit puellam cantāre.*
2. *dīcunt mīlitēs pugnāre.*
3. *scīmus dominum legere.*
4. *audit hostēs venīre.*
5. *scīmus nautam fessum esse.*
6. *sciunt puellam dormīre.*

Exercise 4.3
1. They say that the sailors love inns.
2. The soldier announces that Hannibal has come across the mountains.
3. He says that the Romans have pitched camp near the river.
4. We believe that the barbarians will soon attack Rome.
5. We hope that the general will bring help tomorrow.

Exercise 4.4
1. *dīcit Rōmānōs oppidum oppugnāre.*
2. *dīcit mīlitēs fortiter pugnāre.*
3. *scit hostēs oppidum oppugnātūrōs esse.*
4. *scit hostēs oppidum oppugnāvisse.*
5. *crēdimus mīlitem imperātōrem interfectūrum esse.*

Exercise 4.5
1. To be wounded
2. To be defended
3. To have been drawn up
4. To have been led
5. To have been promised
6. To be killed
7. To have been overcome
8. To be touched
9. To have been given
10. To have been sold

Exercise 4.6
1. *appellārī*
2. *monērī*
3. *portātūrus esse*
4. *nārrāvisse*
5. *oppressūrus esse*
6. *victus esse*
7. *timuisse*
8. *apertus esse*
9. *nūntiātūrus esse*
10. *parāvisse*

Exercise 4.7
1. He says that the city has been attacked.
2. He announces that the soldiers have been killed by the enemy.
3. They know that the general has been warned by the consul.

So you really want to learn Latin...

4. They say that Rome will soon be attacked by the Gauls.
5. We know that songs have been sung by the poets in the forum.

Exercise 4.8
1. *dīcit oppidum aedificārī.*
2. *dīcunt opus iam cōnfectum esse.*
3. *scīmus nāvēs quam celerrimē aedificātum īrī.*
4. *nūntiant multās victōriās ab Hannibale partās esse.*
5. *dīcunt bovēs ad hostēs pulsās* esse.*

*Strictly speaking, *bōs* (masc.) = an ox; *bōs* (fem.) = a cow. An easier word for cow is *vacca, -ae*, fem.

Exercise 4.9
1. He said that the farmers were working in the fields.
2. They said that the sailors loved inns.
3. The soldier announced that Hannibal had come across the mountains.
4. He said that the camp happened to have been pitched near the river.
5. We believed that the barbarians would soon attack the town.

Exercise 4.10
1. *dīxit servōs equōs in agrum dūcere.*
2. *nūntiāvērunt hostēs superātōs esse.*
3. *illa dīcēbat frātrem suum in bellō interfectum esse.*
4. *cēterōs fūgisse forte cognōvimus.*
5. *crēdidī incōlās ferōcēs esse.*
6. *scīmus puellās domī cum mātre forte habitāre.*
7. *nōlī dīcere* dominō tuō servōs omnēs bovēs vēndidisse!*
8. *legātum īn forō cum cōnsulibus rīdēre audīvimus.*

*Dīcō is used when "tell" means "say to".

Exercise 4.11
1. *Resistō* = I resist. To resist is to withstand or oppose.
2. *Certus* = certain. A certainty is something that is taken to be certain.
3. *Cognōscō* = I learn, get to know. Recognition occurs when one realises that one knows someone or something.
4. *Ferōx* = fierce. Ferocious means fierce.
5. *Impetus* = a charge. If one is impetuous, one is rash, akin to one charging headlong.
6. *Honor* = honour. Honorary means conferring honour.
7. *Adversus* = unfavourable. Adverse circumstances are unfavourable ones.
8. *Attonitus* = astonished. Astonished means amazed.
9. *Imperium* = command or empire. Imperial means pertaining to an empire or command.
10. *Faveō* = I favour or support. A favour is a mark of support.

So you really want to learn Latin...

Exercise 4.12
1. *rēgīna sē interfēcit.*
2. *nōlō mē interficere.*
3. *semper nōs dēfendēmus.*
4. *tibĭ legēbās.*
5. *sē docēbit.*
6. *mē legere docuī.*
7. *numquam tē amāvistī.*
8. *fortiter nōs dēfendēmus.*
9. *rēx ipse sē interfēcerat.*
10. *mīlitēs, cūr numquam vōs custōdītis?*

Exercise 4.13
1. The king said that he would overcome the enemy.
2. A certain farmer shouted that he had found gold in the field.
3. The Romans did not know that Hannibal would come across the mountains.
4. The girl heard that she would soon be led into Italy.
5. Two days ago the leader learnt that many horesmen had already set out.
6. The boy said that he hadn't broken the table.
7. O Romans, you will always guard yourselves, won't you?
8. The citizens will defend themselves with swords and spears, won't they?
9. The queen didn't kill herself with a sword, did she?
10. The consuls themselves will fight with the enemy on behalf of the fatherland and will defend it bravely.

Exercise 4.14
1. *negāvit sē Rōmam ventūrum esse.*
2. *negāvimus nōs cibum parāvisse.*
3. *negās tē patrem puerī amāre.*
4. *negāvit sē āram deae parātūram esse.*
5. *iam negāvī mē dōnum amīcō meō datūrum esse.*

Exercise 4.15
1. The father hoped that he would soon return (i.e. hoped to return soon).
2. The daughter of the king promised that she would remain inside the walls (i.e. the daughter of the king promised to remain...).
3. I hope that tomorrow I shall conquer the enemy (i.e. I hope to conquer the enemy tomorrow).
4. We all promised that we would fight bravely for our fatherland (i.e. We all promised to fight bravely...).
5. The soldier promised that he would give a present to his daughters (i.e. The soldier promised to give a present...).

So you really want to learn Latin...

Exercise 4.16

1. *māter iuvenis sē ad rēgem eum ductūram esse prōmīsit.*
2. *Aenēās sē urbem novam in Ītaliā aedificātūrum esse prōmīsit.*
3. *Troiānī sē cibum in īnsulā inventūrōs esse spērāvērunt.*
4. *herī omnēs prōmīsistis vōs librōs domī lectūrōs esse.*
5. *Marce, cūr tē post bellum reditūrum esse prōmīsistī?*

Exercise 4.17

1. *sērāvimus nōs impetum equitum spectātūrōs esse.*
2. *mīlitēs prō honōre Rōmānōrum pugnābant.*
3. *senātus* imperium exercitūs duōbus cōnsulibus dedit.*
4. *cognōvērunt cēterōs mīlitēs mē quaerere.*
5. *Poenōs impetuī nostrō restitisse mē certiōrem fēcit.*

*A better answer might be: *patrēs imperium... dedērunt* (*patrēs* being an honorary title for the senators).

Exercise 4.18

1. He is able
2. They will not want
3. To wish
4. To speak
5. Departing
6. He preferred
7. Having been warned
8. To have arrived
9. To have been carried
10. To be about to be

Exercise 4.19

1. He should have attacked Rome.
2. Hannibal roamed around Italy for fifteen years with an army of 20,000 men.
3. At this time the Carthaginians were losing their grip on Spain, and in 210 B.C. the city of New Carthage fell to the Romans.
4. Publius Cornelius Scipio was responsible for this success.
5. Hasdrubal set off for Italy on the orders of his brother Hannibal.
6. The Romans discovered what Hasdrubal's intentions were by intercepting four secret messages.
7. Gaius Claudius Nero set out to frustrate Hasdrubal's intention of joining up with his brother by joining his consular colleague who was keeping watch over Hasdrubal.
8. He kept his presence secret by not enlarging the size of the camp when his army was joined to that of Marcus Livius Salinator's.
9. In the end the presence of the two consuls was revealed to Hasdrubal by the fact that the trumpet was being sounded twice at supper time.
10. Hannibal learnt that Hasdrubal had been defeated when his brother's head was shot over the walls into his camp.

So you really want to learn Latin...

Chapter 5

Exercise 5.1

1. *ambulat*
2. *ut ambulet*
3. *cadunt*
4. *ut cadant*
5. *facis*

6. *ut faciās*
7. *vulnerantur*
8. *ut vulnerentur*
9. *cōnantur*
10. *ut cōnentur*

Exercise 5.2

1. The woman is hurrying into the fields to find the farmer.
2. The general draws up his forces to fight with the enemy.
3. We shall depart from Rome lest the soldiers kill us.
4. The girl hurries home to prepare the table.
5. They come to the altar to praise the gods.
6. The enemy will pitch camp near the river in order that the Romans may not find water.
7. Hannibal leads his men into the mountains in order that they may make the journey into Italy.
8. The Carthaginians will capture the bodies of the Romans in order that they may send their rings home.
9. The two consuls go towards the river to capture Hasdrubal's camp.
10. You won't come to Rome to see the new temples, will you?

Exercise 5.3

1. *Rōmam ut amīcōs tuōs videāmus vēnimus.*
2. *Rōmā nē mātrem meam videās discessistī.*
3. *nōnne ad urbem ut omnēs librōs meōs legās vēnistī?*
4. *agricola ut frātrem suum aggrederētur* īn forum festīnāvit.*
5. *Hannibal in Hispāniam nūntiōs mittet ut auxilium ā frātre petant.*

*With apologies; this sentence requires the imperfect subjunctive (not covered until next exercise).

Exercise 5.4

1. *ambulāre*
2. *ut ambulārem*
3. *pugnāre*
4. *ut pugnārem*
5. *fugere*

6. *ut fugerem*
7. *discere*
8. *ut discerem*
9. *discēdere*
10. *ut discēderem*

Exercise 5.5

1. *ut docerēmur*
2. *nē spectārētur*
3. *ut timerentur*
4. *nē caperer*

5. *ut sequerentur*
6. *ut cōnārentur*
7. *ut loquerēminī*
8. *ut proficiscerēmur*

So you really want to learn Latin...

Exercise 5.6
1. *in viam cucurrit ut animālia spectāret.*
2. *librum legēbam ut multa dē Rōmānīs cognōscerem.*
3. *pontem custōdiunt, nē ab hostibus capiātur.*
4. *Hannibal, ut suōs in montēs dūceret, profectus est.*
5. *servum mīsī, ut tē adiuvet.*
6. *domum reveniet ut patrem videat.*
7. *in urbem vēnērunt, nē ab hostibus capiantur.*
8. *in urbem vēnērunt, nē ab hostibus caperentur.*
9. *vēnistīne Rōmam, ut cōnsulēs videās?*
10. *Graeciamne adīstī* ut templa vetera vidērēs?*

*N.B. the 2nd person forms of eō in the perfect tense contract: *īstī* and *īstis.*

Exercise 5.7
1. *in urbem ut legere possēmus vēnimus.*
2. *ut tēla in castra portēmus vēnimus.*
3. *ut iterum laetī essēmus ad īnsulam vēnimus.*
4. *quotiēns hūc vēnistī ut aquam in urbem ferās?*
5. *ut iterum prō patriā pugnēmus discessimus.*

Exercise 5.8
1. The Romans prepared ships in order to be able to conquer the Carthaginians.
2. The old man was killed by the soldiers lest he carry food to the citizens.
3. The soldiers were captured lest they return home.
4. We destroyed the ship lest it carry forces to the enemy.
5. I have taught the boy well in order that he may be able to read to me often.

Exercise 5.9
The Romans, who had very many ships, were always able to overcome the Carthaginians in war. They therefore, because they were seeking help from the Greeks, sent ambassadors to the king of Macedonia. However the king, named Philip, was unable to help them. Then the Romans, because they believed they could end the war, advanced into Spain. Publius Scipio with his brother Cnaeus led an army into that land to drive out the Carthaginians. These leaders were killed in the war but Publius's son received (command of) an army from the senate. This man, who for a long time had studied the art of Hannibal, having sent his foot-soldiers around the enemy battle-line, attacked the middle of their column. Moreover he almost destroyed the Carthaginians who had drawn up their forces near a town called Ilipa. Thus Spain, lost by the Carthaginians, was handed over to the Romans.

Exercise 5.10
1. *Odium* = hatred. Odious means hateful.
2. *Libertās* = freedom. Liberty is freedom.

So you really want to learn Latin...

3. *Fīnis* = the end. The finish is the end.
4. *Dēns* = tooth. Dental means relating to teeth.
5. *Studeō* = I study. A student is one who studies.
6. *Stultus* = stupid. To stultify is to cause someone to appear foolish.
7. *Colligō* = I collect. A collection is something that has been collected together.
8. *Oblīvīscor* = I forget. Oblivious means mindless of.
9. *Ōs* = mouth. Oral means relating to the mouth (e.g. oral hygiene).
10. *Causa* = cause. A cause is a reason.

Exercise 5.11

1. Let the soldiers fight bravely on behalf of the fatherland!
2. Let us hurry home to see our mother!
3. Let us seek our friend in the country!
4. Let us listen to the school-master lest he punish us!
5. Let us set out immediately and hurry to Rome!
6. Let him guard the city for five hours!
7. Let them fortify the town with ramparts and walls!
8. "Let all the captured soldiers be killed!" said the leader.

Exercise 5.12

1. *puer dīxit hostēs, quī urbem oppugnārent, cīvēs superātūrōs esse.*
2. *audīvimus imperātōrem, quī in Africā pugnāret, domum venīre velle.*
3. *dīxit senem, quī in viā stāret, patrem cōnsulis esse.*
4. *omnēs scīmus poētās, quī Rōmae habitent, multōs librōs lēgisse.*
5. *dīxērunt mīlitēs, quī in castra impetum facerent, ferōcissimōs esse.*

Exercise 5.13

1. The soldiers said that they would die in order to save the freedom of their friends.
2. He says that the little town, which the Carthaginians want to capture, is fortified with very big ramparts.
3. He said that he wanted to sail to Athens to see the temples, which I have already seen.
4. The leader quickly returned home to announce that he had won a victory.
5. We know that the old man will tell again the story which we have all heard.

Exercise 5.14

1. To be about to slaughter.
2. To have paid the penalty
3. Study the causes of freedom
4. Very stupid
5. Forgetful of freedom
6. After the bones had willingly been collected
7. Into the territory of the state
8. About to forget
9. Without teeth
10. After freedom had been lost

So you really want to learn Latin...

Exercise 5.15
1. The Battle of Ilipa was in 206 B.C. The result of the battle was that Carthage finally lost control of Spain.
2. Scipio crossed into Africa in 204 B.C.
3. Masinissa was the commander of the Numidian cavalry.
4. Masinissa attacked the King of Numidia and captured his capital, Cirta.
5. Masinissa took a shine to the king's daughter, Sophonisba.
6. Sophonisba begged Masinissa not to let her fall into the hands of the Romans. Masinissa responded to this request by marrying her.
7. Scipio did not approve of the marriage.
8. Masinissa managed to keep his promise to his wife by poisoning her!
9. Carthage probably broke its truce because it assumed that, with the return of Hannibal, it would now be able to defeat the Romans.
10. Hannibal's army was in no fit state to take on the Romans.
11. Scipio and Hannibal fought at Zama.
12. The Carthaginian elephants only managed to inflict injuries on the Carthaginians themselves, as they were stampeded by the Roman bugles.
13. After his defeat at Zama, Hannibal was left to supervise the reparation payments to the Romans. However he was then forced to flee from Carthage and ended up helping the king of Bithynia in the latter's war with the king of Pergamum. Eventually the Romans caught up with him and he took poison rather than fall into their hands.
14. Dido's curse had predicted that an heir would rise up from her ashes to bring ruin on Rome. With Hannibal's death, this danger seemed to have passed.

So you really want to learn Latin...

Chapter 6

Exercise 6.1
1. The boy was walking so slowly that he was captured by the school-master.
2. The boy was running so quickly that he arrived at the villa first.
3. He had so great an army that he was easily able to overcome the enemy.
4. The city was being defended so well that it was not captured by the enemy.
5. They have such a general that they fear nothing.

Exercise 6.2
1. *tam fortiter pugnābant ut hostēs vincere possent.*
2. *tam bene cantābat ut in vīllam cōnsulis dūcerētur.*
3. *tot librōs habet ut omnēs legere nōn possit.*
4. *īram cōnsulis adeō timēmus ut ex urbe fugere velīmus.*
5. *tantam domum aedificāvit ut omnēs iam eum laudent.*

Exercise 6.3
1. *Facilis* = easy. Facility means an ease in doing something.
2. *Addō* = I add. Addition is when one adds.
3. *Vīlla* = a country-house. A villa is a country-house.
4. *Fallō* = I deceive. False means untrue and comes from the supine of this verb.
5. *Dubitō* = I doubt. Indubitably means without doubt.
6. *Simul* = at the same time. Simultaneous means at the same time.
7. *Victor* = the victor. If one is victorious one has won.
8. *Exsilium* = exile. Exile is the enforced absence or banishment from one's home.
9. *Fātum* = fate. Fate is inevitable destiny.
10. *Fallō* = I deceive. Fallacious means deceitful or misleading.

Exercise 6.4
1. He quickly ran to the country-house to see his father.
2. He ran so quickly to the country-house that he saw his father.
3. He quickly departed from the city lest he be captured by the guards.
4. He departed from the city city so quickly that he was not captured by the guards.
5. They defended the city well lest it be attacked by the enemy.
6. They defended the city so well that it was not attacked by the enemy.

Exercise 6.5
1.

vīderim	*vīsus sim*
vīderīs	*vīsus sīs*
vīderit	*vīsus sit*
vīderīmus	*vīsī sīmus*
vīderītis	*vīsī sītis*
vīderint	*vīsī sint*

So you really want to learn Latin...

2. tulerim   lātus sim
    tulerīs   lātus sīs
    tulerit   lātus sit
    tulerīmus   lātī sīmus
    tulerītis   lātī sītis
    tulerint   lātī sint

3. dēlēverim   dēlētus sim
    dēlēverīs   dēlētus sīs
    dēlēverit   dēlētus sit
    dēlēverīmus   dēlētī sīmus
    dēlēverītis   dēlētī sītis
    dēlēverint   dēlētī sint

4. spectāverim   spectātus sim
    spectāverīs   spectātus sīs
    spectāverit   spectātus sit
    spectāverīmus   spectātī sīmus
    spectāverītis   spectātī sītis
    spectāverint   spectātī sint

Exercise 6.6

1. They attacked the city so fiercely that they easily captured it.
2. The boy was so tired that he was not punished by the school-master.
3. The Gauls were so terrified that they fled into the wood.
4. Such a great storm arose during the night that many ships were destroyed.
5. Marcus ran so quickly that he soon captured his sister.

Exercise 6.7

1. *tam lentē ambulābat ut mox ā custōdibus capta sit.*
2. *tot vulnera eō diē accēpit ut mortuus sit.*
3. *pugnātum est tam ferōciter ut plūrimī mīlitēs occīsī sint.*
4. *adeō timēbant ut flūmen trānsīre nōllent.*
5. *mūrī urbis tam altī erant ut nēmō eōs ascendere posset.*

Exercise 6.8

1. Do not fight with your allies, Romans!
2. Do not fight with your allies, Romans!
3. Do not walk into the wood, my friend!
4. He ran quickly out of the wood lest he be seen by the lion.
5. He ran so quickly out of the wood that he was not seen by the lion.

So you really want to learn Latin...

Exercise 6.9

1. | trāxissem | tractus essem |
   |---|---|
   | trāxissēs | tractus essēs |
   | trāxisset | tractus esset |
   | trāxissēmus | tractī essēmus |
   | trāxissētis | tractī essētis |
   | trāxissent | tractī essent |

2. | tulissem | lātus essem |
   |---|---|
   | tulissēs | lātus essēs |
   | tulisset | lātus esset |
   | tulissēmus | lātī essēmus |
   | tulissētis | lātī essētis |
   | tulissent | lātī essent |

3. | portāvissem | portātus essem |
   |---|---|
   | portāvissēs | portātus essēs |
   | portāvisset | portātus esset |
   | portāvissēmus | portātī essēmus |
   | portāvissētis | portātī essētis |
   | portāvissent | portātī essent |

4. | vīcissem | victus essem |
   |---|---|
   | vīcissēs | victus essēs |
   | vīcisset | victus esset |
   | vīcissēmus | victī essēmus |
   | vīcissētis | victī essētis |
   | vīcissent | victī essent |

Exercise 6.10

1. When the Romans had fought with Hannibal they conquered him.
2. As soon as Hannibal saw the Romans he drew up his battle-line.
3. Before the general could pitch his camp the enemy led their army into battle.
4. When you came here I showed you the temples.
5. Before you returned home you saw many places.
6. When you had seen the temples you returned home as quickly as possible.
7. After you had seen all the temples I led you into the forum.
8. After you had returned home you gave your mother and father many gifts.
9. As soon as the king had spoken thus we decided to flee.
10. When we had adopted this plan we hurried into the forum.

So you really want to learn Latin...

Exercise 6.11

1. *ubĭ virum īrātum vīdimus, ad silvās statim fūgimus;* or
   cum virum īrātum vīdissēmus, ad silvās statim fūgimus.
2. *postquam vīnum cibumque parāvistī, nōs in vīllam vocāvistī.*
3. *ubĭ ad nostram vīllam vēneris hortōs tibĭ ostendam.*
4. *simul ac aurum invēnimus īn forum id portāvimus.*
5. *priusquam pugnāre poterat castra custōdiēbat.*

Exercise 6.12

1. When we saw the man we fled into the woods.
2. When he had prepared the food he called us into the country-house; or
   When the food had been prepared he called us into the country-house.
3. When he had pitched his camp the leader returned; or
   When the camp had been pitched the leader returned.
4. When we had killed the soldier we fled.
5. When the war had been completed we returned home.
6. When the table had been prepared we ate the food.

Exercise 6.13

1. I am sad because you have departed.
2. I was sad when you were departing.
3. He hurried to Rome because he wanted to see his mother and father.
4. He went into the country-house because he wanted to read all the books.
5. He made a journey into the mountains, since he wanted to conquer Italy.

Exercise 6.14

1. *cum sorōre in hortō lūdit.*
2. *cum imperātor signum dedisset, aciem hostium oppugnāvērunt.*
3. *cum fessus esset, domum ante noctem rediit.*
4. *cum fessus esset, Rōmae septem diēs manēre cōnstituit.*
5. *cum pugnāret cum hostibus, ōre vulnerātus est.*

Exercise 6.15

1. The Carthaginians sent Hannibal into exile since he was not able to overcome the enemy.
2. Hannibal went to a certain king lest he be captured by the Carthaginians.
3. After having waged so many wars on behalf of his country, the bold leader was betrayed by his friends.
4. For a long time he lived in the country-house of a certain king lest he be punished at home.
5. At last he wanted death so much that he killed himself.

So you really want to learn Latin...

Exercise 6.16
1. *Rōmānī Poenōs adeō timēbant ut alium exercitum in Africam mitterent.*
2. *urbem tam bene dēfendēbant ut Rōmānī eam capere nōn possent.*
3. *proximō annō senātus Rōmānus iuvenem, nōmine Cornēlium, mīsit ut Carthāginem oppugnāret.*
4. *cum hic imperātor maximum exercitum habēret, mūrōs urbis perrumpere poterat.*
5. *paucōs diēs hostēs tam ferōciter sē dēfendere poterant ut Cornēlius eōs superāre nōn posset.*

Exercise 6.17
1. *cōnsul fīet.*
2. *Rōmam idcírcō vēnit ut cōnsul fieret.*
3. *cōnsul factus est.*
4. *cōnsul fīet.*
5. *postquam cōnsul factus est ex urbe discessit.*

Exercise 6.18
1. *arce captā cōpiae Rōmānae hostēs fugāvērunt.*
2. *tot mīlitibus interfectīs cēterī pācem accipere coāctī sunt.*
3. *imperātor Rōmānus hostēs adeō ōderat* ut omnia aedificia eōrum dēlēret.*
4. *hōc factō gēns Pūnica numquam Rōmānōs terruit.*
5. *Carthāgine dēlētā, Rōma tot gentēs regēbat ut urbs maxima fieret.*

*For *ōdī* see p.86.

Exercise 6.19
1. The Romans became so proud that everyone feared them.
2. When the Romans had overcome the Carthaginians, they destroyed their city lest they ever be conquered by them again.
3. A certain master set fire to his country-house lest it be captured by the Carthaginians.
4. So many women and men were led to Rome that there were very many slaves in the city.
5. A Roman citizen called Tiberius Gracchus was so afraid of the slaves that he hurried into the senate and warned the senators.
6. He wanted to give fields (i.e. land) to the citizens so that they could live in the country-side.
7. His brother, called Gaius, also wanted to help the citizens.
8. Gaius, however, was killed with many of his friends lest the customs of the Romans be destroyed.
9. The wisdom of the Romans was very great; our wisdom, however, is very small!
10. After the enemy had been defeated, the brave soldier was made leader.

So you really want to learn Latin...

Exercise 6.20
1. Rome continued to distrust Carthage because they considered her a threat to their domination of the western Mediterranean.
2. In 150 B.C. the Romans noticed that the Carthaginians were re-arming, in contravention of the treaty of 201 B.C.
3. Marcus Cato was particularly insistent that Carthage should be destroyed.
4. The Roman demand that they leave Carthage and go to live in a remote, inland area in Tunisia, led the Carthaginians to prepare for war.
5. In 147 B.C. the Romans sent Publius Cornelius Scipio Aemilianus to sort out the war in Carthage.
6. 50,000 Carthaginians were captured and sold into slavery.
7. The city itself was dismantled, stone by stone.
8. *Dēlenda est Carthāgō* means Carthage must be destroyed.

So you really want to learn Latin...

Chapter 7

Exercise 7.1
1. *servō imperāvit ut domum venīret.*
2. *mīlitibus imperāvit ut pugnārent.*
3. *nōs monuērunt nē domum venīrēmus.*
4. *nōbīs imperāvērunt ut pugnārēmus.*
5. *servus ā dominō petīvit ut puerōs domum mitteret.*
6. *imperātor cōpiīs imperāvit ut castra aedificent.*
7. *hostēs nōs hortātī sunt ut fugiāmus.*
8. *mē monuit ut manērem.*
9. *cūr rogātī sumus ut pugnēmus?*
10. *quis vōbīs imperāvit, puellae, ut ad urbem redīrētis?*

Exercise 7.2
1. Regulus ordered the Romans to fight with the enemy again.
2. After the attack had been made the general ordered his men to withdraw.
3. I have persuaded my friend to live with his mother.
4. They have warned us to adopt a plan.
5. The leader persuaded his men not to use so many arrows.
6. The master warned the small boys to hide their fear.
7. Meanwhile the ambassador was begging the senate that the prisoners be freed.
8. Some citizens advised the king to fight.
9. Hannibal encouraged his forces to make an attack on the Romans.
10. This soldier, sent by the Carthaginians, begged the senate not to make peace.

Exercise 7.3
1. *Rapiō* = I seize. If one is rapt with wonder, one is seized by wonder.
2. *Neglegō* = I neglect. To neglect is to ignore or to overlook.
3. *Sanguis* = blood. Sanguine means confident (blood was thought to predominate over the other humours).
4. *Mereor* = I deserve. Merit is excellence which deserves honour or reward.
5. *Vēndō* = I sell. A vendor is someone who sells.
6. *Pereō* = I die. To perish is to die.
7. *Ad + ōrō* = I pray to. To adore is to worship or to revere highly.
8. *Inimīcus* = enemy. Inimical means hateful.
9. *Opprimō* = I overwhelm. Oppressive means overwhelming.
10. *Quiēs* = quiet. Quiet means lack of noise, calm.

Exercise 7.4
1. *mē Rōmam venīre iussit.*
2. *mē Rōmam venīre vetuit.*
3. *mē rūrī manēre voluit.*
4. *mē cum Poenīs pugnāre nōluērunt.*
5. *rēx eum effugere prohibuit.*

So you really want to learn Latin...

Exercise 7.5

1. The leader gave orders to the soldiers that their battle-line be drawn up in that place.
2. The consul ordered the soldiers to draw up their battle-line.
3. The Roman citizens advised me not to do that.
4. After we had heard this we ordered the girl to run home as quickly as possible.
5. The father forbade the boys to read the master's books.

Exercise 7.6

1. *puellae quae in viā erant pulcherrimae erant.*
2. *castra prope flūmen posuit.*
3. *agricolās quī in agrō erant sciēbāmus.*
4. *gladiī in mēnsā positī puellam terrēbant.*
5. *Hannibal Rōmānōs prope oppidum superāvit.*

Exercise 7.7

1. He watched the girl while he was near the inn.
2. Near the river Romulus saw the city.
3. Hannibal destroyed the forces on the plain.
4. In the forum the consul praised the gods.
5. In the country-house, everyone heard the noise.

Exercise 7.8

1. Everyone knew why the citizen, called Sulla, had come to Rome.
2. The citizens asked each other what they would do.
3. The Romans asked whether Sulla would kill all his enemies.
4. Sulla was asking the citizens why they had fought in the war.
5. You do want to know when he will return to Rome, don't you?
6. The girl asked her brother whether he was afraid or not.
7. He asked the old man whether he would hurry home or remain in the country-side.
8. We ask the boy whether he has seen the temples or not.
9. The leader asked his men whether they would pitch camp near the river or in the wood.
10. He did not know whether the Romans or the Carthaginians had won the victory.

Exercise 7.9

1. *rogāvimus cūr vēnisset.*
2. *cognōscere volumus quis advēnerit.*
3. *sciunt cūr interfectus sit.*
4. *eum rogābō quandŏ discessūrus sit.*
5. *imperātōrem rogāvī quot mīlitēs in pugnam dūxisset.*
6. *ā senibus quaesīvimus utrum pugnam vīdissent necne.*
7. *ā mātre vestrā quaerētis utrum domum adīre an Rōmae manēre velit.*
8. *nesciēbat utrum Rōmānī an hostēs castra prope oppidum posuissent.*
9. *nescīmus utrum virum amēs necne.*
10. *agricolam rogāvērunt utrum bovēs in agrum an īn silvam dūxisset.*

So you really want to learn Latin...

Exercise 7.10

The people of Italy, after the Carthaginians had been defeated, did not wish to obey the Roman senate. Therefore, under the leadership of Marius, the Roman forces waged a war with the inhabitants of Italy. Marius, having won many victories, begged the senate that he himself should lead the Roman army for longer. The senate, however, because it was afraid to give Marius such great power, ordered another leader, called Lucius Porcius Cato, to lead the Romans on his own.

This Cato, who was consul at that time, was not skilled in war and was unable to overcome the enemy. Therefore at last the senate was forced to give the inhabitants the vote.

Exercise 7.11

1. He sent the boys into the city to buy bread.
2. The consul sent the soldiers into the country-house of the old man to seize his riches.
3. The sad woman sent the young men to bury the old man.
4. The leader will make a charge at the enemy in order more easily to overcome them.
5. There are some who always fear the dangers of the city.

Exercise 7.12

1. *nūntiōs mīsērunt quī victōriam populō Rōmānō nūntient.*
2. *gladium rapuit quō custōdēs facilius interficeret.*
3. *Hannibal dignus est quī Rōmānōs vincat.*
4. *sunt quī semper amīcōs opprimant.*
5. *nōn est is quī mōrēs patriae neglegat.*

Exercise 7.13

1. *dīvitiīs iūdicis raptīs, ille īn silvās fūgit.*
2. *corpore sorōris prope flūmen sepultō, domum cum amīcīs rediit.*
3. *carmen pulchrum cantāns per viās oppidī ambulābat.*
4. *Poenī, postquam dē montibus dēscendērunt, castra Rōmānōrum oppugnāvērunt.*
5. *suōs ad arma vocātōs cōnsul hostēs aggredī iussit;* or
   postquam suōs ad arma vocāvit cōnsul eīs ut hostēs aggliderentur imperāvit.

Note how an ablative absolute cannot be used here (as explained on p.20).

Exercise 7.14

1. Leaving their weapons, the enemy fled from the Romans.
2. Seizing the wine, the farmer hurried out of the inn.
3. His crime neglected by all, the wicked citizen returned home.
4. Because his riches had been seized by the enemy, the old man was forced to sell his country-house.
5. When the city was captured, all the citizens perished.

Exercise 7.15

1. While he was walking, he suddenly heard a voice.
2. We want you to come here, provided that you remain for a few days.
3. The Romans fought bravely until the battle was finished.
4. The Romans waited near the river for the enemy to return.
5. While the poet was writing, the slaves were singing.

So you really want to learn Latin...

Exercise 7.16

After the enemy had at last been overcome, Sulla killed very many citizens so that he would not be overwhelmed by them. He terrified the Roman people so much that at last all his enemies were unwilling to remain at home. For Sulla ordered his guards to capture his enemies, seize their riches, and slaughter them. He often asked who had helped Marius. Then the guards were ordered to look for those citizens and kill them.

Afterwards Sulla became dictator. For three years he managed the affairs of the city until at last, leaving the city, he went to his country-house in Campania to enjoy the quiet in the country-side.

Exercise 7.17

1. *ab eō quaesīvimus cūr tot cīvēs Rōmae periissent.*
2. *dīxit Sullam urbem intrāvisse et inimīcōs cēpisse.*
3. *eum ōrāverant nē senēs opprimeret, sed frūstrā.*
4. *tot interfectī sunt ut mox Sulla Rōmae sōlus regeret.*
5. *incolās Ītaliae ut Rōmānōs adiuvārent hortātus est.*
6. *omnēs sciēbāmus cūr auxilium eōrum vellet.*
7. *urbe captā custōdēs suōs dīvitiās cīvium rapere iussit.*
8. *eī quī Sullae pārēre nōlēbant periērunt.*
9. *inimīcī Sullae ab urbe fūgērunt nē interficerentur.*
10. *quis scit num cīvēs hunc scelestum oppressūrī sint.*

Exercise 7.18

1. The Romans fought against Jugurtha, King of Numidia, between 111 and 105 B.C.
2. Jugurtha had upset his brother by driving him from the throne.
3. Marius led the Roman army in the war against Jugurtha. The Romans won.
4. "Marius's mules" was the name given to the soldiers under Marius's command.
5. The Roman senate did not wish Marius to continue to lead the army because it feared that his power was growing too great.
6. Lucius Porcius Cato took over command of the army and was singularly unsuccessful.
7. As a result of their success in the war the Italians were granted Roman citizenship.
8. When Sulla marched into Rome, he (a) reversed the grants of citizenship and (b) outlawed Marius.
9. In 87 B.C. Cornelius Cinna was driven from Rome for trying to restore the grants of citizenship. He raised an army of peasants, joined up with Marius, and re-entered the city at the head of an army.
10. In 83 B.C. civil war broke out.
11. Sulla held the office of dictator for three years and terrorised the people of Rome during this time, particularly his enemies.
12. Sulla may have grown tired of public life; he may have considered that he had achieved his ends; he may have feared retribution if he continued to oppress the people; he may have had a genuine respect for the republic of Rome and its institutions, despite his apparent tyrannical behaviour.

So you really want to learn Latin...

Chapter 8

Exercise 8.1

1. *sī tū laetus es, ego quoque laetus sum.*
2. *sī hostēs vincās, tē laudem.*
3. *sī incolās Ītaliae superāvissēs, Rōmam cēpissēs.*
4. *sī Marius Rōmae habitāret, inimīcī eius timērent.*
5. *nisi eōs vīcissēmus, fūgissēmus.*
6. *sī vīllam vendās, multās dīvitiās accipiās.*
7. *sī quam celerrimē ambulāveris, crās adveniēs.*
8. *nisi epistolam lēgissēs, nihil dē amīcō cognōvissēs.*
9. *nisi Rōmam celeriter vēneris, patrem meum nōn vidēbis.*
10. *nisi crās cīvēs cōnsulī pāruerint, poenās dabunt.*

Exercise 8.2

1. If you were to come here, you would see my mother.
2. If you don't come here you will not see my mother.
3. If the ambassador had sought peace, we should have sent him home immediately.
4. If you order my soldiers to attack the town, they will attack it.
5. If you were to order my soldiers to attack the town, they would not obey you.
6. The Romans would have overcome the enemy if they had not pitched their camp near the river.
7. If the farmer had prepared his fields well, we should all have had food.
8. If you do not work, poor citizens, you will not be able to have corn.
9. You will live for a long time if you avoid your worst enemies.
10. If you come here at dawn you will see the sailors sailing out of the harbour.

Exercise 8.3

ōlim imperātor Rōmānus, nōmine Sulla, Rōmae regere volēbat. sī ā Mariō superātus esset, tot cīvēs nōn interfēcisset. postquam tamen urbem intrāvit, omnibus ut sibī pārērent imperāvit et custōdibus ut omnēs inimīcōs interficerent. cēterī terrēbātur cum nescīrent utrum sē interfectūrus esset necne. fortasse rēx factus esset sī Rōmae diūtius mānsisset. sed rūs profectus ad vīllam rediit et multōs annōs habitābat.

Exercise 8.4

1. *sī herī hostēs cōnspexissēs, eōs ē patriā expulissēmus (pepulissēmus).*
2. *sī superfuisset nunc senex esset.*
3. *hostēs etiam nunc adessent nisi imperātōrem dē adventū eōrum monuissēs.*
4. *sī mihī illud dīxisset barbam eius rapuissem.*
5. *sī castra intrābitis*, vōs gladiīs interficiēmus.*
6. *sī hostēs aquilās nostrās capiant, domum redīre nōn possīmus.*

*Note the future tense; this is very much a threat (see p. 80)!

So you really want to learn Latin...

Exercise 8.5

1. My daughter is seventeen years old.
2. How old is your father?
3. How happy I should be if you would sing that song again!
4. He will take your goods if you are not careful.
5. He would still be alive if he hadn't rushed alone into the battle.
6. We asked that soldier whether he wanted to guard the eagle.
7. How swift the enemy cavalry would be if we had sold them our horses!
8. If he had wanted glory he would have waged war in Africa for longer.
9. If my father were to be kinder, perhaps I should come to Rome.
10. I shall bury his body if he is killed.

Exercise 8.6

1. *Mora* = delay. A moratorium is a suspension of payments.
2. *Adveniō* = I arrive. An advent is an arrival.
3. *Barba* = beard. A barber cuts hair (and beards!).
4. *Cōnspiciō* = I catch sight of. Something that is conspicuous can easily be seen.
5. *Benignus* = kind. Benign means favourable or kindly.
6. *Caveō* = I am cautious. Cautious means careful.
7. *Cantō / canō* = I sing. A canticle is a type of song.
8. *Dūrus* = hard. Durable means long-lasting.
9. *Aquila* = eagle. Aquiline means hooked, like an eagle's bill.
10. *Custōdiō* = I guard. A custodian is a guard.

Exercise 8.7

1. *quamquam hostēs superāvimus, cīvēs nunc exercitum suum timent.*
2. *hostēs numquam timēbimus, quamvīs in bellō fortēs sint.*
3. *etsī domum nunc cuccureris, mātrem patremque nōn vidēbis.*
4. *etsī cum eō pugnēs, nōn possīs eum superāre.*
5. *etsī oppidum noctū oppugnāvissētis, nōn cēpissētis.*

Exercise 8.8

1. Although they want to fight, they will not be able to defeat us.
2. However much they may wish to fight, they will not be able to defeat us.
3. We returned to the camp although we had not conquered the enemy.
4. He led his forces back onto the plain although they feared the dangers of war.
5. Even if you had chosen him as consul, you would now fear him.

Exercise 8.9

1. Although they do not wish to fight, the enemy are hateful to us.
2. Although he may not wish to fight, Hannibal is a cause of anxiety to the Romans.
3. Even if he had not attacked Rome, the Roman citizens would not have been helpful to him.
4. A king was always hateful to the Roman citizens.
5. After he had conquered the enemy the leader was no longer a disgrace to his soldiers.

So you really want to learn Latin...

Exercise 8.10
1. *Rōmam venīre timēnt.*
2. *timent nē hostēs Rōmam veniant.*
3. *timēbāmus nē mīlitēs Poenōs nōn superārent.*
4. *timēbat nē māter sē nōn vidēret.*
5. *verēbāmur ut frāter noster rediisset.*

Exercise 8.11
1. *imperātor mīlle nāvēs parāvit ut cum exercitū trāns mare nāvigāret.*
2. *dux hostium quīnque mīlia peditum et duo mīlia equitum īnstrūxit.*
3. *cōnsul cum mīlle peditibus et plūrimīs equitibus ad urbem contendit.*
4. *servī, quī tria tantum mīlia peditum habēbant, cōnsulēs adeō timēbant ut fugerent.*
5. *mīlitēs, quī quīnque mīlia passuum contenderant, fessī erant.*

Exercise 8.12
1. The old man bought his country-house for a lot of *sestertii*.
2. He sold the slave to his friend for one thousand *denarii*.
3. We greatly value the poems of the Greek poets.
4. The soldiers marched for seven miles.
5. The Roman citizens valued their freedom very highly.

Exercise 8.13
1. After dinner the poet began to sing.
2. Who remembers the beautiful daughters of the old man?
3. "I do not love this woman," said the young man, "but nor do I hate her."
4. He said that he remembered all the dangers of war.
5. The Romans were always saying that they hated the Carthaginians.

Exercise 8.14
1. *nōs omnēs Poenōs ōdimus ut Rōmae hostēs.*
2. *agricola mūrum circum agrōs aedificāre coeperat.*
3. *scīmus cīvēs Sullam sīc ōdisse ut omnēs mīlitēs hostēs ōdisse.*
4. *iuvenis verba sapientia amīcōrum meminerat.*
5. *virtūtem magnam imperātōris nōs semper meminerimus.*

Exercise 8.15
1. Spartacus was a Thracian-born gladiator.
2. He led a slave rebellion in 73 B.C.
3. Spartacus's army grew to around 70,000.
4. The two consuls sent to deal with Spartacus were defeated in battle.
5. Command was given to Crassus with an army of six legions.
6. Crassus wanted to defeat Spartacus before the arrival of Pompey, his rival.
7. After Spartacus's death, 6,000 of his followers were crucified along the Appian Way.
8. Yes!

So you really want to learn Latin...

GE

GREEK

**A quick beginners' course for
holidaymakers and businesspeople**

Course writer: David Hardy
Language consultant: John Pavlides
Programme presenters: Christina Coucounara
Yorgos Yannoulopoulos
Producer: Christopher Stone

BBC Books

Get by in Greek
A BBC Radio Course
First broadcast in April 1983

Published to accompany a series of programmes
prepared in consultation with the
BBC Continuing Education Advisory Council

Acknowlegements
The staff and customers of
Compendium Bookshop, Plaka, Athens

Cover designed by Peter Bridgewater and Annie Moss

Published by
BBC Publications,
a division of BBC Enterprises Ltd,
Woodlands, 80 Wood Lane,
London W12 0TT

ISBN 0 563 39962 7
First published in 1983
Reprinted 1983 (twice), 1985, 1986 (twice), 1987 (twice)
This edition first published in 1995
© The Authors and
BBC Enterprises Limited 1983

Printed and bound in Great Britain
by Clays Ltd, St Ives plc
Cover printed by Clays Ltd, St Ives plc

Contents

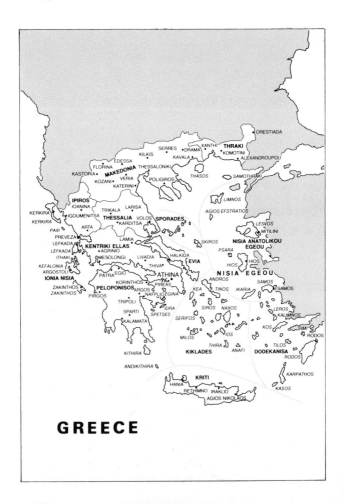

GREECE

The course...
and how to use it

The BBC *Get By in Greek* course provides basic, practical knowledge to all those who want to learn Greek, whatever their language abilities. The book contains five chapters and a reference section while the cassettes contain five corresponding units as well as a pronunciation guide.

The cassettes

☐ are based on real-life conversations specially recorded in Athens (Αθήνα), so that you'll get used to hearing everyday Greek right from the start

☐ concentrate on the language you'll need in particular situations, such as shopping, finding your way around, booking a hotel room, ordering coffee, and so on

☐ help you to understand the Greek that's likely to be said to you in these situations, and to recognise key words and phrases, so that you can pick out the information you need, even when you don't understand every word

☐ give you plenty of opportunity to practise the words and phrases you'll need to say

☐ include a list of words from the pronunciation guide on pp. 58–61 of this book so that you can hear the sounds of Greek as you look at the alphabet.

The book includes

☐ the key words and phrases for each chapter

☐ the texts of the conversations in the order you'll hear them in the cassettes

☐ short explanations of the language

☐ useful background information about Greece

☐ self-checking exercises to do after each chapter and a short test on the whole course at the end

☐ a reference section containing a guide to the pronunciation of the Greek alphabet, with a list of words to practise written both in the Greek alphabet and with English letters. This section also contains extra language notes, useful addresses, the key to the exercises and a Greek-English word list (with pronunciations)

☐ a list of words and phrases for use in emergencies.

To make the most of the course

☐ The way you use the course will depend on you and on whether you're using the cassettes. Here are some suggestions:

☐ *The Greek alphabet:* if possible, look at the pronunciation guide on p 58 and practise saying the words in the list out loud several times. If you have the cassettes, listen to these words at the end of Cassette 2 when you practise.

☐ *Before each cassette unit:* look at the key words and phrases at the beginning of each chapter. You'll find them written in English letters as well as Greek, and you should practise saying them out loud. Read through the conversations out loud several times, with someone else if possible, and check the pronunciation and meaning of any words or phrases you don't know in the word list at the end of this book. To help you further, you'll find the alphabet written out on page 59 and across the top of each page of the word list.

☐ *During each cassette unit:* listen to the conversations without looking at the book and concentrate on the sounds of the language. When you're asked to repeat a word or phrase, try saying it out loud, and confidently; this will help you to remember the expressions and to learn to say them with the proper stress. The pauses may seem a little short at first; if so, stop the tape with the pause button.

☐ *After each cassette unit:* read through the conversations out loud again. You may find it useful to imitate the conversations phrase by phrase, using the pause button to stop the tape. Then work through the language explanations and the exercises in the book.

☐ *When you go to Greece or Cyprus:* take this book and a phrase book, such as the BBC's *Greek Phrase Book*, with you.

1 Meeting people

Key words and phrases

To say and understand

Γειά σας Yásas	Hello or goodbye *(formal)*
Χαίρετε Hérete	Hello or goodbye *(formal)*
Γειά σου Yásoo	Hello or goodbye *(informal)*
Τί κάνετε; TECANITA Ti kánete?	How are you? *(formal)*
Τί κάνεις; Ti kánis?	How are you? *(informal)*
(Πολύ) καλά ευχαριστώ (Polí) kalá efharistó	(Very) well thank you

E FERI STO
THANK YOU

To say

Ένα καφέ παρακαλώ 'Ena kafé parakaló	A coffee please
Ένα τσάϊ παρακαλώ 'Ena tsáï parakaló	A tea please
Μία μπύρα παρακαλώ Mía bíra parakaló	A beer please

To understand

Τί θα πάρετε; Ti tha párete?	What will you have?
Τί καφέ θέλετε; Ti kafé thélete?	What sort of coffee do you want?

Conversations

These can be heard on the cassettes. Check the pronunciation and meaning of new words in the Greek-English word list (p 70).

The four conversations you'll hear right at the beginning of unit 1 all occur later in the course. If you want to follow them at this stage, you'll find them written out on p 48.

Helloes and goodbyes

Woman	Γειά σας.
Man	Γειά σας.
Man	Χαίρετε.
Woman	Χαίρετε.
1st woman	Γειά σου.
2nd woman	Γειά σου.
Nikos	Γειά σου Αγγελική.
Angeliki	Γειά σου Νίκο.

Good morning, good evening, goodnight, goodbye

Woman	Καλημέρα.
Man	Καλημέρα.
Man	Καλησπέρα.
Woman	Καλησπέρα.
Man	Καληνύχτα.
Woman	Καληνύχτα.
Man	Καλημέρα.
Man	Καλημέρα σας.
Woman	Καλημέρα.
Woman	Καλημέρα σας.
Man	Καλησπέρα.
Woman	Καλησπέρα.
Man	Καλησπέρα σας.
Woman	Καλησπέρα.
Woman	Καληνύχτα.

εννιά **9**

| Man | Καληνύχτα. |
| Woman | Καληνύχτα σας. |

Woman	Αντίο.
Woman	Αντίο.
Man	Αντίο σας.

How are you?

Mrs Smith	Καλησπέρα κύριε Παππά.
Mr Pappas	Καλησπέρα σας κυρία Σμίθ.
	Τί κάνετε;
Mrs Smith	Καλά ευχαριστώ. Εσείς;
Mr Pappas	Πολύ καλά ευχαριστώ.

Maria	Γειά σου Καίτη.
Katy	Γειά σου Μαρία. Τί κάνεις;
Maria	Μιά χαρά. Εσύ;
Katy	Καλά.

Ordering a coffee . . .

NEHARA – EVERY THINGS FINE
121
CALA – WELL

Waiter	Τί θά πάρετε;
Customer	Ένα καφέ παρακαλώ.
Waiter	Τί καφέ θέλετε;
Customer	Μέτριο.
Waiter	Αμέσως.

| Waiter | Χαίρετε. Τί θά πάρετε; |
| Customer | Ένα ζεστό νές μέ γάλα παρακαλώ.* |

*A hot instant coffee with milk, please

. . . or a tea

Waiter	Χαίρετε. Τί θά πάρετε;
Customer	Ένα τσάι μέ γάλα παρακαλώ.
Waiter	Αμέσως.

Waiter	Χαίρετε. Τί θά πάρετε;
Customer	Ένα τσάι μέ λεμόνι.
Waiter	Αμέσως.

. . . or a beer

Waiter	Τί θά πάρετε;
Customer	Μία μπύρα παρακαλώ.
Waiter	Μικρή ή μεγάλη;
Customer	Μικρή.
Waiter	Αμέσως.

Explanations

Saying hello and goodbye

γειά σας or χαίρετε – you can use either expression at any time of day, to mean either 'hello' or 'goodbye', when addressing one person rather formally, or when speaking to more than one person

γειά σου is the informal version of γειά σας, used when you're speaking to just one person

καλημέρα and καλημέρα σας literally 'good day', are used like the English 'good morning', until lunch time. During the afternoon, use χαίρετε.

καλησπέρα and καλησπέρα σας 'good evening' (from about 5.30 onwards)

καληνύχτα and καληνύχτα σας 'goodnight'

αντίο and αντίο σας 'goodbye' – at any time of day

Adding σας makes all the above slightly more formal.

Please and thank you

ευχαριστώ is 'thank you'   *EFERISTO*
παρακαλώ is 'please'. Also 'not at all', 'don't
mention it', as a reply to ευχαριστώ.   *EFAROSTOW*
                          PARACALOR

Gestures

Greeks use many facial and hand gestures to
communicate without actually speaking. You
should look out especially for the gesture meaning
'no': the head is tilted upwards and backwards,
though this is often reduced to a raising of the
eyebrows. For 'yes' the head is tilted downwards
and to one side. When the head is shaken from side
to side, rather like the English 'no' gesture, this
implies a question: this gesture is often
accompanied by a rotating of the hand, with thumb
and first two fingers extended.

How to address people

κύριε to a man
κυρία to a married or older woman
δεσποινίς to a younger woman

If a Greek name ends in ς, this is usually left off
when you speak to the person directly.
Γιώργος becomes Γιώργο, Νίκος becomes Νίκο, etc.

Saying how you are

Τί κάνετε; and τί κάνεις; 'how are you?'

Τί κάνετε; is the formal way to ask, and τί κάνεις; the
informal. People will often move quickly to using
the informal τί κάνεις; but you should use the
formal τί κάνετε; with someone you are meeting for
the first time.

Εσείς; and εσύ; '(and) you?' Εσείς is formal – a
response to τί κάνετε; and εσύ is the reply to the
informal τί κάνεις;

Πολύ καλά ευχαριστώ 'very well thank you'

Μιά χαρά 'fine' – a less formal reply, often used between friends

Ordering coffee, tea, etc

Τί θά πάρετε; 'what will you have?' Other expressions waiters use frequently are **τί θέλετε;** 'what do you want?' and **παρακαλώ;** '(yes) please?'

καφέ is the general word for coffee. If you're ordering Greek coffee, you'll need to ask for **ένα σκέτο** (a coffee without sugar), **ένα μέτριο** (a medium coffee) or **ένα γλυκό** (a sweet coffee).

Τί μπύρα θέλετε; Μικρή ή μεγάλη; Notice the pattern **τί . . . θέλετε;** 'what (kind of) . . . do you want?' The choice here is **μικρή ή μεγάλη;** 'small or large?'

αμέσως 'immediately', 'right away' – it's what waiters will say once they've taken your order or to let you know you've caught their eye. *ZESTO – HOT*
MENGALA – WITH MILK

Masculine, feminine and neuter

In Greek, words for things are divided into three groups – masculine, feminine and neuter. When you're ordering anything or saying what you want, the word for 'a', or 'one' is **μία** if you're talking about a feminine word, and **ένα** if it's a masculine or a neuter word: so it's **μία μπύρα** but **ένα καφέ** and **ένα ούζο**. See the reference section on p 62 for more about masculine, feminine and neuter words.

ENA ZESTO NESS MEGALA
HOT WHITE COFFEE

Accents

When Greek words are written in small letters, they have an accent on the part of the word to be stressed. Traditionally there are three accent signs ´ ` ˆ but they all have the same effect and it has now been decided to use just a single accent. In this book, the single accent ´ is used, always on the stressed part of the word. You will sometimes see two other signs above letters at the beginning of words ᾿ ῾. These do not affect the way the word is pronounced, and have now been abandoned. They are not used in this book.

Numbers

0	μηδέν	1	ένα	2	δύο
3	τρία	4	τέσσερα	5	πέντε

(One is sometimes μία, and three and four are sometimes τρεις and τέσσερεις – see reference section p 64.)

Questions

The Greek question mark is like an English semicolon. Τί κάνετε; 'how are you?'

Exercises

1 Choose an appropriate greeting for each of the following situations:

i   You come down from your hotel room in the morning and say 'hello' to the receptionist:

   α Γειά σας
   β Αντίο σας
   γ Καλησπέρα
   δ Καληνύχτα σας

ii   You meet your friend Nikos by chance, and say 'hello':

   α Χαίρετε
   β Γειά σου
   γ Καλημέρα σας
   δ Καληνύχτα

iii   You go into a shop in the middle of the morning and say 'good morning' to the shopkeeper:

   α Καληνύχτα σας
   β Καλημέρα σας
   γ Καλησπέρα
   δ Αντίο σας

iv You meet your business associate for early evening drinks. To greet him, you say:

  α Γειά σου
  β Καλημέρα
  γ Καλησπέρα
  δ Αντίο

v After dinner with friends, you say 'goodnight':

  α Γειά σου
  β Καλημέρα σας
  γ Καλημέρα
  δ Καληνύχτα σας

2 Practise reading these greetings out loud.

  α Γειά σας
  β Γειά σου
  γ Χαίρετε
  δ Καλημέρα
  ε Καλησπέρα
  ζ Καληνύχτα
  η Αντίο σας

Which one would you use:
a only in the evening...
b only in the morning..
c only late at night...
d only with someone you know quite well............
   ....

3 You're introduced to a businessman at the hotel. How do you ask 'how are you?'

  α Τί κάνετε;
  β Τί κάνεις;
  γ Καλά ευχαριστώ

He says he's well thank you, and asks how you are. What do you reply?

  α Καλά. Εσύ;
  β Πολύ καλά ευχαριστώ
  γ Τί κάνετε;

You meet someone you've met several times before who asks how you are. How do you say, 'Fine thanks, how about you?'

α Καλά ευχαριστώ
β Τί κάνετε;
γ Μιά χαρά. Εσύ;

Which of the following is he likely to answer?

α Τί κάνετε;
β Τί κάνεις;
γ Καλά

4 Choose an appropriate answer to these questions:

Τί θά πάρετε;	α Μία μπύρα παρακαλώ
	β Καλά ευχαριστώ
	γ Χαίρετε
Τί κάνετε;	α Καλά ευχαριστώ
	β Γειά σας
	γ Ένα τσάϊ μέ λεμόνι
Τί καφέ θέλετε;	α Ένα τσάϊ μέ γάλα
	β Μέτριο
	γ Μία μπύρα
Μικρή ή μεγάλη;	α Ένα ζεστό νές
	β Ένα καφέ παρακαλώ
	γ Μικρή
Τί κάνεις;	α Μιά χαρά
	β Καλά ευχαριστώ. Εσείς;
	γ Γειά σου

Worth knowing

Where to get a drink and a cake

You can get coffee, tea, soft drinks and alcoholic drinks, ice-cream and a cake at a ζαχαροπλαστείο, a cafe where people meet to have a leisurely chat over a drink. In summer it will invariably have tables and chairs outside on the pavement as well as inside.

You can also get a coffee or a drink at a **καφενείο**: traditionally this is a place where men meet and talk, or play cards or backgammon (**τάβλι**).

Drinks and snacks are also served at a **ΣΝΑΚ ΜΠΑΡ** or a **ΜΠΥΡΑΡΙΑ**

As for tipping, it's common to leave a few drachmas for the waiter.

Greek coffee is very strong and served in small cups. The sugar is added before it is made, and you have to order it sweet, medium, or without sugar. You can also get instant coffee anywhere in Greece, and some places will serve French, Italian or American coffee.

Tea is often served in a pot with a jug of milk (if you've asked for it) and sugar. Occasionally, your tea may come ready-poured.

A large beer is about half a litre, and a small beer about a third.

Drinks, cakes and ice-creams

coffee

ένα καφέ *black coffee*
ένα σκέτο *a Greek coffee without sugar*
ένα μέτριο *a medium Greek coffee*
ένα γλυκό *a sweet Greek coffee*
ένα νές *instant coffee*
ένα φραπέ *iced coffee, shaken and sipped through a straw*
ένα εσπρέσσο *an espresso*
ένα καπουτσίνο *a capuccino*
ένα γαλλικό καφέ *a French coffee*
ένα αμερικάνικο καφέ *an American coffee*

ENI TIE MEL A MORNY TEA WITH LEMON

tea	ένα τσάϊ μέ γάλα a tea with milk
ENI TIE MELAMORNY	ένα τσάϊ μέ λεμόνι a tea with lemon
soft drinks	μία πορτοκαλάδα an orangeade
	μία λεμονάδα a lemonade
	μία κόκα κόλα a cola
	ένα χυμό πορτοκάλι an orange juice
	ένα χυμό λεμόνι a lemon juice
	μία γρανίτα a sorbet
alcoholic drinks	μία μπύρα a beer *MIRA BÉRA / BEER*
MÉCRE – SMALL	ένα ούζο an ouzo
MERIALE – LARGE	ένα κονιάκ a brandy
cakes	μία πάστα a cake
	ένα μπακλαβά a pastry with nuts and honey
ice-cream	ένα παγωτό an ice-cream
	κρέμα plain
	σοκολάτα chocolate
	παρφέ mixed
	σικάγο often chocolate and plain ice-cream, with cream and chocolate sauce

2 Going shopping

Key words and phrases

To say

Ἕνα μπουκάλι ρετσίνα παρακαλῶ
'Ena boukáli retsína parakaló

A bottle of retsina please

Μήπως ἔχετε αυγά;
Mípos éhete avgá?

Do you have any eggs?

Μισόκιλο ντομάτες
Misókilo domátes

Half a kilo of tomatoes

Ἕνα τέταρτο
'Ena tétarto

A quarter of a kilo

Πόσο κάνει;
Póso káni?

How much does it cost?

Πόσο κάνουνε;
Póso kánoone?

How much do they cost?

To understand

Τί θέλετε;
Ti thélete?

What do you want?

Πόσα θέλετε;
Pósa thélete?

How many do you want?

Τίποτ'ἄλλο;
Típot'állo?

Anything else?

Ὁρίστε
Oríste

Here you are

Μάλιστα
Málista

Certainly

δεκαεννιά **19**

Conversations

Ordering two beers . . .

Waiter	Τί θά πάρετε;
Customer	Δύο μπύρες παρακαλώ.
Waiter	Αμέσως.

. . . and two medium coffees

Waiter	Τί θά πάρετε;
Customer	Δύο καφέδες παρακαλώ.
Waiter	Τί καφέδες θέλετε;
Customer	Μέτριους.
Waiter	Αμέσως.

Buying a bottle of retsina . . .

Customer	Ένα μπουκάλι ρετσίνα παρακαλώ.
Shopkeeper	Μάλιστα. CERTAINLY
Customer	Πόσο κάνει;
Shopkeeper	Ογδόντα δραχμές.

. . . a quarter of ham

Customer	Καλησπέρα.
Shopkeeper	Καλησπέρα. Τί θέλετε;
Customer	Ένα τέταρτο ζαμπόν.
Shopkeeper	Ναί. YES ¼ of HAM

. . . half a kilo of tomatoes

Customer	Μισόκιλο ντομάτες παρακαλώ.
Shopkeeper	Μάλιστα.
Customer	Πόσο κάνουνε;
Shopkeeper	Τριάντα πέντε δραχμές.
Customer	Ευχαριστώ.
Shopkeeper	Κι εγώ ευχαριστώ.

. . . a map of Athens

Customer	Μήπως έχετε χάρτες;
Girl in kiosk	Μάλιστα. Τί χάρτη θέλετε;

Customer	Τής Αθήνας παρακαλώ*.
Girl in kiosk	Ορίστε.
Customer	Πόσο κάνει;
Girl in kiosk	Πενήντα δραχμές.
Customer	Ευχαριστώ.
Girl in kiosk	Παρακαλώ.

*Of Athens please.

. . . and half a dozen eggs

Customer	Καλημέρα σας.
Shopkeeper	Καλημέρα. Τί θέλετε;
Customer	Μήπως έχετε αυγά;
Shopkeeper	Μάλιστα. Πόσα θέλετε;
Customer	Έξι. _EX₁ SIX_
Shopkeeper	Τίποτ΄άλλο;
Customer	Όχι, ευχαριστώ. _NO THANK-YOU_

OSHI AFERISTO

Filling the car (see also p 45)

PETROL PLEASE

Customer	Βενζίνη παρακαλώ. _BENZINE PARAKALOR_
Attendant	Σούπερ ή απλή;
Customer	Σούπερ. _SUPER_
Attendant	Πόσο;
Customer	Πεντακόσιες δραχμές.

APLI - ORDINARY 4*

PORSO - HOW MUCH

Explanations

Ordering more than one

When you want to ask for more than one of
anything, you usually have to change the ending of
the word. **Μπύρα** becomes **μπύρες**, **καφέ** becomes
καφέδες, **μέτριο** changes to **μέτριους**, **τσάϊ** to **τσάϊα**
and **ούζο** to **ούζα.** But some foreign words don't
change at all: **νές** and **κονιάκ** for example. The way
the word changes depends on the way it ends, and
whether it's masculine, feminine or neuter. You can
find the pattern set out on page 63 of the reference
section.

One, two, three, four and five

'One' can be either **μία** or **ένα**. 'Two' is always **δύο**, but three and four change, and can be either **τρείς** and **τέσσερεις** or **τρία** and **τέσσερα**. When you're ordering, or asking for things, you count **μία, δύο, τρείς, τέσσερεις** with feminine words, **ένα, δύο, τρείς, τέσσερεις** with masculine words, and **ένα, δύο, τρία, τέσσερα** with neuter words. All the numbers that end in one, three or four change in this way. **Πέντε** 'five' doesn't change. Again, the reference section on page 63 should help to make all this clear.

Numbers 1-100

1	ένα/μία	11	έντεκα		
2	δύο	12	δώδεκα	20	είκοσι
3	τρία/τρείς	13	δεκατρία/ δεκατρείς	30	τριάντά
4	τέσσερα/ τέσσερεις	14	δεκατέσσερα/ δεκατέσσερεις	40	σαράντα
5	πέντε	15	δεκαπέντε	50	πενήντα
6	έξι	16	δεκαέξι	60	εξήντα
7	εφτά	17	δεκαεφτά	70	εβδομήντα
8	οχτώ	18	δεκαοχτώ	80	ογδόντα
9	εννιά	19	δεκαεννιά	90	ενενήντα
10	δέκα			100	εκατό

[Handwritten margin annotations: ENNA, THEO, TREA, DESERA, PENDA, EXI, EFTA, OCTO, ENIYA, VECA, ENDICA, THOTHECA, ECOS, TRANDA, SARANDA, PENENDA, EXINDA, OVANDA, ENERMIN, EKATO, VECA]

(You will sometimes hear slightly different variations of some of the numbers: for example, **επτά** for **εφτά** and **εννέα** for **εννιά**.)

Up to a hundred, numbers are combined exactly as in English:

είκοσι ένα *twenty one*
τριάντα τρία *thirty three*
σαράντα τέσσερα *forty four*
πενήντα εφτά *fifty seven*
ογδόντα δύο *eighty two*

How many do you want?

πόσα θέλετε; is 'how many do you want?' You will

sometimes hear πόσους θέλετε; or πόσες θέλετε; instead. It depends on whether what you're asking for is masculine, feminine or neuter. πόσο θέλετε; is 'how much do you want?'

How much does it cost?

πόσο κάνει; is 'how much does it cost?' when you're buying a single item. It's πόσο κάνουνε; 'how much do they cost?' when you're paying for more than one thing (and a kilo of tomatoes, for example, is more than one thing). You'll often hear πόσο κάνουν; for πόσο κάνουνε;

The drachma

The Greek unit of currency is the δραχμή 'drachma', or δραχμές for more than one. Because δραχμή is a feminine word, you'll hear μία δραχμή, τρείς δραχμές, τέσσερεις δραχμές, τριάντα μία δραχμές, πενήντα τρείς δραχμές and so on. Often, though, people will miss off the δραχμές and you'll just hear a number: τριάντα τέσσερεις, εβδομήντα τρείς, and so on.

Saying 'yes' and 'no'

Μάλιστα and ναί are two common words for 'yes'. You may also hear πώς and βεβαίως or βέβαια 'certainly, of course'. Όχι is 'no'.

In the shop

When you go into a shop, you may be asked τί θέλετε; 'what do you want?', μάλιστα; 'yes?', παρακαλώ; or ορίστε; Often, though, the shopkeeper will wait for you to speak first. Τίποτ'άλλο; is 'anything else?' When you've finished shopping and said ευχαριστώ the shopkeeper may reply κι εγώ ευχαριστώ 'thank *you*'.

ένα μπουκάλι ρετσίνα – there's no word for 'of' in expressions like this. You'll also ask for **μισόκιλο ντομάτες** and so on.

Exercises

1   The waiter in a **ζαχαροπλαστείο** asks for your order. Choose the correct way to order:

a two coffees   α δύο καφές
                             β δύο καφέ
                             γ δύο καφέδες

b three beers	α τρείς μπύρα
	β τρείς μπύρες
	γ τρία μπύρες
c four teas	α τέσσερεις τσάι
	β τέσσερεις τσάϊες
	γ τέσσερα τσάϊα
d three medium coffees	α τρείς μέτριους
	β τρία μέτριους
	γ τρία μέτριο
e two ouzos	α δύο ούζους
	β δύο ούζο
	γ δύο ούζα

2   You go into a small shop and the shopkeeper says **Καλημέρα. Τί θέλετε;** Does he mean:
a   Good evening. What do you want?
b   Good morning. What do you want?
c   Good morning. How are you?

You want to ask for a quarter of a kilo of ham. Do you say:
α   μισόκιλο ζαμπόν
β   ένα τέταρτο ζαμπόν
γ   ζαμπόν παρακαλώ

He gives you the ham and says **τίποτ΄άλλο;** Is he saying:
a   There you are
b   That's 50 drachmas
c   Anything else?

You want to know if he's any tomatoes. Do you say:
α   μισόκιλο ντομάτες
β   μήπως έχετε ντομάτες;
γ   ένα τέταρτο ντομάτες

When you get the tomatoes, you want to know how much they cost. Do you say:

α Πόσο κάνουνε;
β Πόσο κάνει;
γ Τί κάνετε;

He says they're **πενήντα οχτώ δραχμές.** Is that:

a eighteen drachmas
b fifty eight drachmas
c eighty five drachmas

3 You're shopping for a picnic. Order the following items:

i   half a kilo of tomatoes...
ii   a quarter kilo of ham ....
iii six eggs ....
iv   a bottle of retsina..

Ντομάτες	80	τό κιλό
ρετσίνα	85	τό μπουκάλι
φέτα	150	τό κιλό
Κασέρι	145	τό κιλό
Ζαμπόν	120	τό κιλό
αυγά	5	

4 Look at the price list above and work out the price of each of the items you have just ordered in Exercise 3. How much do you have to pay altogether? Tomatoes and some other items are priced by the kilo.

Worth knowing

Shopping for food

There is a growing number of supermarkets in Athens and the larger towns. Look for the sign **ΣΟΥΠΕΡΜΑΡΚΕΤ** or **ΥΠΕΡΑΓΟΡΑ.** In smaller towns and villages, look for the grocer's shop with the sign **ΠΑΝΤΟΠΩΛΕΙΟΝ.**

You can buy bread **(ψωμί)** at the shop with the sign **ΑΡΤΟΠΟΙΕΙΟΝ** or **ΑΡΤΟΠΩΛΕΙΟΝ** (though when you're asking the way to the baker's you need to ask for **o φούρνος**).

Kiosks

Περίπτερα, 'kiosks', are open much longer hours than the shops, and sell a surprisingly wide range of goods, including toilet articles such as tooth-paste, soap, disposable razors and so on.

The post office

The post office is the **ΤΑΧΥΔΡΟΜΕΙΟΝ**. The post office colour is yellow, and the abbreviation **ΕΛΤΑ** (**Ελληνικά Ταχυδρομεία** – Greek post offices) is often used.

The word for stamp is **γραμματόσημο** (**γραμματόσημα** for more than one) and if you want to buy stamps 'for England', it's **γιά τήν Αγγλία.**

Telephones

You can make phone calls from many of the kiosks, or from telephone boxes with the sign **ΤΗΛΕΦΩΝΟΝ.** Boxes with this sign on a blue background are for local calls only; inter-city phones have an orange background. You can also make long distance calls, or send a telegram, from the **OTE** – the Greek telecommunications service.

The main office in central Athens is open 24 hours. Regional offices close late evening.

The chemist's

The sign for the chemist's is **ΦΑΡΜΑΚΕΙΟΝ**: many chemists will diagnose minor complaints.

For emergency first aid, you can call Athens First Aid Station at 166.

The butcher's

You can buy meat at a **ΚΡΕΟΠΩΛΕΙΟΝ**. The cuts of meat are different from those in England but, in general terms, **μοσχάρι** is veal, **χοιρινό** is pork, and **αρνάκι** is lamb. For mince, ask for **κυμά**. Sausages **λουκάνικα** are not sold at butcher's shops, but where you see the sign **ΑΛΛΑΝΤΙΚΑ**. For steak you should ask for **μπόν φιλέ**. Chops or cutlets are **μπριζόλες.**

The final **N** on many of the shop signs etc is not pronounced in everyday speech. You will *see* **ΦΑΡΜΑΚΕΙΟΝ, ΤΑΧΥΔΡΟΜΕΙΟΝ, ΕΣΤΙΑΤΟΡΙΟΝ, ΤΗΛΕΦΩΝΟΝ** but you *say* **φαρμακείο, ταχυδρομείο, εστιατόριο, τηλέφωνο.**

Weights

The basic measure of weight is the kilo – **τό κιλό.** Half a kilo is **μισόκιλο,** and a quarter is **ένα τέταρτο** (three quarters is **τρία τέταρτα**). Liquids are also sold by weight, as well as by the bottle (**τό μπουκάλι).**

3 Booking a hotel room

Key words and phrases

To say

Μήπως έχετε δωμάτια;
Mípos éhete thomátia?
Do you have any rooms?

Έχω κλείσει ένα δωμάτιο
'Eho klísi éna thomátio
I've reserved a room

Ένα δίκλινο
'Ena thíklino
A double

Θέλω νά χαλάσω πενήντα λίρες
Thélo na haláso penínda líres
I want to change fifty pounds

To understand

Τί δωμάτιο θέλετε;
Tí thomátio thélete?
What room do you want?

Γιά πόσες μέρες;
Ya póses méres?
For how many days?

Δυστυχώς δέν έχουμε
Thistihós thén éhoome
Unfortunately we don't have

Είμαστε γεμάτοι
'Imaste yemáti
We're full

Τό όνομά σας παρακαλώ
To ónomásas parakaló
Your name please

Τό διαβατήριό σας παρακαλώ
To thiavatíriósas parakaló
Your passport please

Υπογράψτε παρακαλώ
Ipográpste parakaló
Sign please

εἴκοσι εννιά **29**

Conversations

Booking a double room

Tourist	Καλημέρα.
Receptionist	Καλημέρα σας.
Tourist	Μήπως έχετε δωμάτια;
Receptionist	Βεβαίως. Τί δωμάτιο θέλετε;
Tourist	Ένα δίκλινο.
Receptionist	Μάλιστα. Μέ μπάνιο;
Tourist	Ναί.
Receptionist	Γιά πόσες μέρες;
Tourist	Τρείς.
Receptionist	Εντάξει. Τό διαβατήριό σας παρακαλώ.
Tourist	Ορίστε.
Receptionist	Ευχαριστώ.

Finding the hotel full

Tourist	Μήπως έχετε δωμάτια;
Receptionist	Δυστυχώς δέν έχουμε.
	Είμαστε γεμάτοι.

A room booked in advance

Tourist	Καλησπέρα σας.
Receptionist	Καλησπέρα.
Tourist	Έχω κλείσει ένα δωμάτιο.
Receptionist	Τό όνομά σας παρακαλώ;
Tourist	Σμίθ.
Receptionist	Τό δωμάτιό σας είναι
	στό δεύτερο όροφο.*
Tourist	Τί αριθμό;
Receptionist	Διακόσια πέντε.
Tourist	Ευχαριστώ.
Receptionist	Παρακαλώ.

*Your room is on the second floor.

Changing travellers' cheques

Tourist	Χαλάτε traveller's cheques;
Bank clerk	Ναί. Βεβαίως.

Tourist	Θέλω νά χαλάσω πενήντα λίρες.
Bank clerk	Ευχαρίστως. Υπογράψτε παρακαλώ.
Tourist	Ορίστε.
Bank clerk	Τό διαβατήριό σας παρακαλώ.
Tourist	Ορίστε.
Bank clerk	*(Checks the tourist's passport and counts out the money.)* Ορίστε.
Tourist	Ευχαριστώ. Γειά σας.
Bank clerk	Γειά σας.

Explanations

Hotel rooms

A single room is **ένα μονόκλινο,** a double **ένα δίκλινο** and a room with three beds **ένα τρίκλινο.** A **δίκλινο** will have two beds by the way. If you want a double bed, you should ask for a room **μέ διπλό κρεββάτι.**

μέ μπάνιο is 'with a bath', **μέ ντούς** is 'with a shower'.

For how long?

γιά πόσες μέρες; 'for how many days?' You may also hear **πόσο θά μείνετε;** 'how long are you going to stay?', to which the answer is **δύο/τρείς μέρες** etc. **μία εβδομάδα** is 'one week'.

Numbers over 100

100	εκατό	600	εξακόσια
200	διακόσια	700	εφτακόσια
300	τριακόσια	800	οχτακόσια
400	τετρακόσια	900	εννιακόσια
500	πεντακόσια	1000	χίλια

2000	δύο χιλιάδες
3000	τρείς χιλιάδες
4000	τέσσερεις χιλιάδες, and so on

The numbers 200, 300, 400 . . . up to 1000 change their ending depending on whether the things you are counting are masculine, feminine or neuter. If you're talking about drachmas, they're feminine and it's **διακόσιες, τριακόσιες, τετρακόσιες δραχμές** up to a thousand **χίλιες.**

When these higher numbers are combined, there is no word for 'and' as there is in English.

Some prices in drachmas:

πεντακόσιες οχτώ   508
οχτακόσιες σαράντα τρείς   843
χίλιες τριακόσιες είκοσι μία   1,321
δεκατρείς χιλιάδες εφτακόσιες ενενήντα έξι   13,796

But room numbers end in **-κόσια**:
διακόσια πέντε   205
τριακόσια είκοσι   320
πεντακόσια οχτώ   508

Being told they don't have any rooms

δέν is 'not': **έχουμε δωμάτια** 'we have rooms', but **δέν έχουμε δωμάτια** 'we don't have rooms'.

Your room is . . .

στό δεύτερο όροφο 'on the second floor'. **Πρώτο** is 'first', **τρίτο** 'third', **τέταρτο** 'fourth' and **πέμπτο** 'fifth'.

Exercises

1   The conversation below is one you might have if you were trying to book a room in a hotel. The receptionist's part is written out for you. Work out your part of the conversation:

You	*(hello)* ....
Receptionist	Καλησπέρα σας
You	*(do you have any rooms?)* ....
	....
Receptionist	Βεβαίως. Τί δωμάτιο θέλετε;
You	*(a single please)* ....

Receptionist	Μέ μπάνιο;
You	*(yes)*.....................
Receptionist	Γιά πόσες μέρες;
You	*(four)*.....................
Receptionist	Εντάξει
You	*(how much does it cost?)*.................
Receptionist	Χίλιες διακόσιες δραχμές
You	*(OK)*.....................
Receptionist	Τό διαβατήριό σας παρακαλώ
You	*(here you are)*.....................
Receptionist	Ευχαριστώ

2 Read these requests for accommodation out loud. Which of them suits the groups of people listed below?

α Ένα δίκλινο γιά τρείς μέρες
β Ένα μονόκλινο γιά δύο μέρες
γ Ένα τρίκλινο γιά μία μέρα
δ Ένα δίκλινο καί ένα μονόκλινο γιά εφτά μέρες
ε Ένα δίκλινο καί ένα τρίκλινο γιά τέσσερεις μέρες

i *Mr and Mrs Lingris, visiting Athens for three days*
ii *Mr Smith, in town on business for two days*
iii *Mr and Mrs Hornsby and their 4 year old daughter Salli, staying overnight*
iv *Mr and Mrs Brown and their 17 year old son Peter, on holiday for a week*
v *Five friends touring Greece*

3 You've just come back to the hotel and want to ask for your key. Practise saying the following room numbers out loud.

a 205 ....
b 305 ....
c 310 ....
d 410 ....
e 507 ....

4   You want to change money at the bank.
Practise the following sentence, filling in the gap
with the amounts of money listed below:

α   θέλω νά χαλάσω (50) ....λίρες
β   θέλω νά χαλάσω (20) ....λίρες
γ   θέλω νά χαλάσω (100) ....λίρες
δ   θέλω νά χαλάσω (25) ....λίρες
ε   θέλω νά χαλάσω (40) ....λίρες

Worth knowing

Hotels

For detailed information on hotels, and for many
other aspects of a visit to Greece, you should
consult the Greek National Tourist Organisation
(address on p 66), which also has offices in Greece.

Hotels are classified L (luxury) and **A, B, Γ, Δ, E** (A,
B, C, D, E). At the height of the summer season
you'd be advised to book in advance. The prices
quoted are usually for the room, not per person.

You can also stay in a room in a private house,
though you will have to arrange this on the spot.
The local office of the tourist police **ΤΟΥΡΙΣΤΙΚΗ
ΑΣΤΥΝΟΜΙΑ** will give you advice on this, as on
many other situations you'll meet as a tourist.

There are a number of camping sites in Greece
offering modern facilities, some of which have
bungalow-huts as well as space for tents, caravans
and camping vans.

Banks

Banks are open Monday to Friday from 8.00 am to
1.30 pm and most will change traveller's cheques
or cash a personal cheque for up to £50 if
accompanied by the appropriate cheque card. Look
out for the sign **ΣΥΝΑΛΛΑΓΜΑ** 'exchange'.

The Greek unit of currency is the **δραχμή**
sub-divided into 100 **λεπτά**, though inflation over
the years has made these **λεπτά** almost worthless.
(You may occasionally see a 50 **λεπτά** piece.)

Banknotes

1,000 drachmas – χιλιάρικο
  500 drachmas – πεντακοσάρικο
  100 drachmas – κατοστάρικο
   50 drachmas – πενηντάρικο

Coins

   50 drachmas – πενηντάρικο
   20 drachmas – εικοσάρικο
   10 drachmas – δεκάρικο
    5 drachmas – τάληρο
    2 drachmas – δίφραγκο
    1 drachma – φράγκο
   ½ drachma (50 λεπτά) – πενηνταράκι

4 Finding your way around

Key words and phrases

To say

Συγγνώμη Signómi	Excuse me
Πού είναι τό μουσείο; Poo íne to moosío?	Where is the museum?
Υπάρχει ξενοδοχείο εδώ κοντά; Ipárhi xenothohío ethó kondá?	Is there a hotel nearby?
Τί ώρα φεύγει τό καράβι; Ti óra févyi to karávi?	What time does the boat leave?
Τί ώρα φτάνει; Ti óra ftáni?	What time does it arrive?
Από πού φεύγει τό λεωφορείο; Apo poo févyi to leoforío?	Where does the bus leave from?
Γιά τό Σούνιο πάει αυτό; Ya to Soónio pái aftó?	Does this go to Sounio?
Πιό αργά παρακαλώ Pyó argá parakaló	Slower please

To understand

Αριστερά, δεξιά, ευθεία Aristerá, thexiá, efthía	Left, right, straight on
Τό πρώτο στενό αριστερά Tó próto stenó aristerá	The first street on the left
Στή γωνία Stí gonía	At the corner

τριάντα εφτά **37**

Conversations

Asking the way to the museum . . .

Man	Συγγνώμη. Πού είναι τό μουσείο παρακαλώ;
Girl	Τό δεύτερο στενό αριστερά καί τό πρώτο δεξιά,
Man	Ευχαριστώ.
Girl	Παρακαλώ.

. . . and Sindagma square

1st Man	Πού είναι τό Σύνταγμα παρακαλώ;
2nd Man	Θά στρίψετε αριστερά στή γωνία, καί μετά τό τρίτο στενό δεξιά.
1st Man	Πιό αργά παρακαλώ.
2nd Man	Θά στρίψετε αριστερά στή γωνία, καί μετά τό τρίτο στενό δεξιά.
1st Man	Ευχαριστώ.
2nd Man	Παρακαλώ.

Finding out if there's a hotel nearby

1st Man	Συγγνώμη. Υπάρχει ξενοδοχείο εδώ κοντά;
2nd Man	Ναί, βέβαια. Ευθεία, στό δεύτερο στενό δεξιά.
1st Man	Ευχαριστώ.
2nd Man	Παρακαλώ.

Asking about boat times

Customer	Τί ώρα φεύγει τό καράβι γιά τή Σάμο;
Travel agent	Επτάμιση τό πρωί.
Customer	Καί τί ώρα φτάνει;
Travel agent	Πέντε τό απόγευμα.
Customer	Εντάξει.

Catching the bus to Sounio

Tourist	Από πού φεύγει τό λεωφορείο γιά τό Σούνιο;

1st Man	Από τήν πλατεία Αιγύπτου*.
	*From Egypt Square
Tourist	Γιά τό Σούνιο πάει αυτό;
2nd Man	Μάλιστα.
Tourist	Τί ώρα φεύγει;
2nd Man	Σέ δέκα λεπτά περίπου.*
	*In about ten minutes
Tourist	Δύο γιά τό Σούνιο παρακαλώ.
	Πόσο κάνουνε;
Conductor	Διακόσιες εξήντα δραχμές.

Explanations

Asking the way

When you stop someone to ask them the way, you can say **συγγνώμη** or **μέ συγχωρείτε** 'excuse me', or simply **παρακαλώ.**

To ask the way to somewhere specific, you ask **πού είναι . . . . ;** followed by the name of the place you're looking for. The word for 'the' is sometimes **ο**, sometimes **η** and sometimes **τό** depending on whether the word itself is masculine, feminine or neuter: **ο φούρνος** 'the baker's', **η τράπεζα** 'the bank' and **τό μουσείο** 'the museum'. (See reference section, page 62.) To ask more generally if there's, say, a hotel nearby, it's **υπάρχει ξενοδοχείο εδώ κοντά;** If you wanted a bank, it would be **υπάρχει τράπεζα εδώ κοντά;**

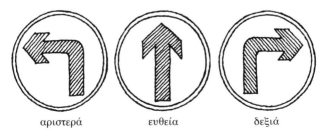

αριστερά   ευθεία δεξιά

Understanding the reply

You probably won't understand every word of the reply, so listen out for the key words and phrases: **αριστερά, δεξιά, ευθεία** 'left, right, straight on', **στενό** 'street' (though you will also hear **δρόμος**), **στή γωνία** 'at the corner' (also 'on the corner') and **πρώτο, δεύτερο, τρίτο** 'first, second, third'.

Enquiring about public transport

Τί ώρα is 'what time?' You can ask **τί ώρα φεύγει;** 'what time does it leave?' and **τί ώρα φτάνει;** 'what time does it arrive?' **Από πού φεύγει;** is 'where does it leave from?' All three questions can be combined with the words for bus **(τό λεωφορείο)**, boat **(τό καράβι)**, train **(τό τραίνο)** and plane **(τό αεροπλάνο)**, and you can ask **τί ώρα φεύγει τό αεροπλάνο;** or **τί ώρα φτάνει τό τραίνο;** or **από πού φεύγει τό καράβι;** and so on.

γία τή Σάμο is 'for Samos'.

To make sure that you've found the right bus, boat or whatever you can ask **γιά (τό Σούνιο) πάει αυτό;** 'does this go to (Sounio)?' (See reference section page 62.)

Clock time

The exact hours are **μία, δύο, τρείς, τέσσερεις**, and so on up to twelve o'clock which is **δώδεκα**. For the half hours, you'll sometimes hear **μία καί μισή, δύο καί μισή** 'one and a half', 'two and a half', and so on. You'll also often hear the following expressions:

1.30	μιάμιση	7.30	εφτάμιση
2.30	δυόμιση	8.30	οχτώμιση
3.30	τρεισήμιση	9.30	εννιάμιση
4.30	τεσσερεισήμιση	10.30	δέκα καί μισή★
5.30	πεντέμιση	11.30	εντεκάμιση
6.30	εξίμιση	12.30	δωδεκάμιση

★you'll rarely hear **δεκάμιση**

For minutes past the hour, it's **καί**: and so **μία καί δέκα, μία καί τέταρτο** and **μία καί είκοσι** are ten past one, quarter past one and twenty past one. For minutes to the hour, it's **παρά**: and so **μία παρά δέκα, μία παρά τέταρτο** and **μία παρά είκοσι** are ten to one, a quarter to one and twenty to one.

'At' a certain time is **στή** when the hour is one but otherwise it's **στίς**. This means it's **στή μία καί τέταρτο** 'at a quarter past one' but **στίς πέντε παρά είκοσι** 'at twenty to five'. **Σέ** is 'in' and the word for minutes is **λεπτά**: **σέ δέκα λεπτά** 'in ten minutes', **σέ μισή ώρα** 'in half an hour', **σέ ένα τέταρτο** 'in a quarter of an hour' and **σέ μία ώρα** in an hour.

On Greek timetables the initials **ΠΜ (πμ)** and **ΜΜ (μμ)** are the equivalent of AM (am) and PM (pm). **Τό πρωί** is 'in the morning' and **τό απόγευμα** 'in the afternoon/early evening'.

Exercises

1   You are at the spot marked on the map over the page. First read each of the questions out loud, and then choose which set of directions is the one that will get you where you want to go.

Questions

α   Πού είναι τό μουσείο παρακαλώ;
β   Πού είναι τό ξενοδοχείο ''Αλφα' παρακαλώ;
γ   Πού είναι τό Σύνταγμα παρακαλώ;

Directions

i   Τό δεύτερο στενό αριστερά καί τό πρώτο δεξιά
ii   Θά στρίψετε αριστερά στή γωνία, καί μετά τό δεύτερο στενό δεξιά
iii Θά πάτε ευθεία καί θά στρίψετε στό τρίτο στενό αριστερά
iv   Ευθεία, τό τρίτο στενό δεξιά
v   Τό πρώτο στενό αριστερά καί τό πρώτο δεξιά

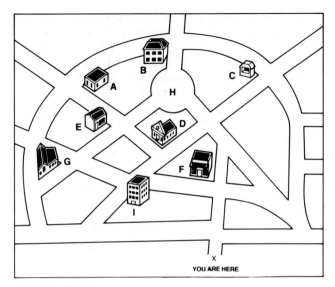

YOU ARE HERE

KEY TO MAP

A cake-shop ζαχαροπλαστείο
B bank τράπεζα
C kiosk περίπτερο
D post-office ταχυδρομείο
E chemist φαρμακείο
F taverna ταβέρνα
G museum μουσείο
H Sindagma Square τό Σύνταγμα
I Hotel Alpha ξενοδοχείο ''Άλφα'

2   Ask if there is one of the following places nearby:

i   post office (ταχυδρομείο) ....
....

ii   bank (τράπεζα) ....
....

iii   kiosk (περίπτερο) ....
....

iv   chemist's (φαρμακείο) ....
....

v ζαχαροπλαστείο ....

....

vi ταβέρνα ....

3 Match these prices with the tickets

α Τριάντα   δ Τριάντα πέντε
β Εξήντα πέντε   ε Δεκαπέντε
γ Εκατό   ζ Πενήντα

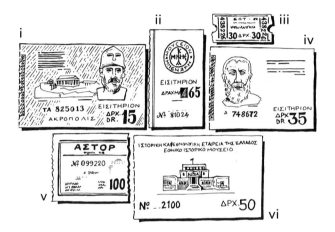

4 You want to visit the island of Rhodes by boat.
Fill in the gaps in the conversation.

You *(what time does the boat leave for*
Rhodes? – γιά τή Ρόδο).....................

....

Travel agent Οχτώ τό πρωί
You *(what time does it arrive?)*...............

....

Travel agent Τέσσερεις τό απόγευμα
You *(OK – two please)*...........................

....

Travel agent Μάλιστα
You *(how much are they?)*.......................

....

Travel agent	Χίλιες τετρακόσιες δεκαπέντε
You	*(Here you are)*.....................................
	....
Travel agent	Ευχαριστώ

Worth knowing

Getting around

By bus

There is a wide network of buses covering the whole of Greece, and there are also inter-city buses operated by the railway company **(ΟΣΕ)**.

In Athens some local routes are served by trolley buses as well as ordinary buses. There is a flat fare on both. A one-man bus will have the sign **ΧΩΡΙΣ ΕΙΣΠΡΑΚΤΟΡΑ** 'no conductor' on the front; and the entrances and exits are clearly marked **ΜΟΝΟΝ ΕΙΣΟΔΟΣ** and **ΜΟΝΟΝ ΕΞΟΔΟΣ**.

By underground

Athens is also served by the ηλεκτρικός or underground. It has a single line, running from the port of Piraeus via Omonia Square to the suburb of Kifisia. Fares are cheap, and it is a convenient way of travelling between Athens and the port of Piraeus.

By boat

The Greek islands are served by boats, most of which start from Piraeus near Athens. There are four classes: πρώτη 'first', δεύτερη 'second', τουριστική 'tourist', and τρίτη 'third'.

By train

There are two rail networks, linking Athens with the Peloponnesos and the north of Greece. Neither is extensive, and buses are usually quicker.

By air

Olympic Airways operates domestic flights to many parts of Greece. The main office is in Sindagma Square in Athens.

By car

Many international car hire firms are represented in Greece and there are also numerous other companies. Βενζίνη 'petrol' is sold in litres, and there are 2 grades: σούπερ (roughly equivalent to 4 star) and απλή (2 star). The Greek motoring organisation is ΕΛΠΑ and its address is:

Odos Mesogion 2-4   Odos Amerikis 6
Athens   Athens
(Tel: 779-1615)   (Tel: 363-8632)

Road Assistance – Tel: 104

5 Eating out

Key words and phrases

To say

Τό κατάλογο To katálogo	The menu
Γιά ορεκτικά τί έχετε; Ya orektiká ti éhete?	What do you have for starters?
Φέρτε μας μερικούς μεζέδες Férte mas merikoós mezéthes	Bring us some hors d'oeuvres
Τό λογαριασμό To logariasmó	The bill

To understand

Τί θά φάτε; Ti tha fáte?	What will you eat?
Τί θά πιείτε; Ti tha pyíte?	What will you drink?
Καθήστε Kathíste	Take a seat

Conversations

Ordering lunch

Customer	Γειά σας.
Waiter	Χαίρετε.
Customer	Τό κατάλογο παρακαλώ.
Waiter	Αμέσως . . . Τί θά φάτε;
Customer	Ένα κοτόπουλο μέ πατάτες καί μία χωριάτικη.*

Waiter	Τί θά πιείτε;
Customer	Μισόκιλο κρασί καί νερό.
Waiter	Αμέσως.

*A chicken with potatoes and a mixed salad.

Paying the bill

Woman	Τό λογαριασμό παρακαλώ.
Waiter	Αμέσως . . . Διακόσιες είκοσι δραχμές.
Woman	Ορίστε, ευχαριστώ.
Waiter	Εγώ ευχαριστώ. Γειά σας.

Getting a toasted sandwich . . .

Snack-bar owner	Παρακαλώ;
Customer	Ένα τόστ μέ ζαμπόν καί τυρί παρακαλώ.
Snack-bar owner	Καθήστε.

. . . and a cheese pie

Snack-bar owner	Παρακαλώ;
Customer	Μία τυρόπιττα παρακαλώ.
Snack-bar owner	Θά τή φάτε εδώ, ή θά τή πάρετε μαζί σας;*
Customer	Εδώ.

*Are you going to eat it here or are you going to take it with you?

Eating in a taverna

Waiter	Τί θά φάτε;
Customer	Γιά ορεκτικά τί έχετε;
Waiter	Τζατζίκι, κολοκυθάκια, μελιτζάνες, χταποδάκι, τυροπιττάκια, σαλάτα χωριάτικη.*
Customer	Ωραία. Φέρτε μας μερικούς μεζέδες.
Waiter	Μετά τί θά φάτε;

Customer	Μία μπριζόλα μοσχαρίσια
	καί ένα σουβλάκι.
Waiter	Μάλιστα.

*A yoghurt and garlic salad, courgettes, aubergines, octopus, small cheese pies, mixed salad.

The following conversations occur at the beginning of unit 1.

Buying a cup of coffee

Waiter	Τί θά πάρετε;
Customer	Ένα καφέ παρακαλώ.
Waiter	Τί καφέ θέλετε;
Customer	Μέτριο.
Waiter	Αμέσως.

Going shopping

Customer	Ένα μπουκάλι ρετσίνα
	παρακαλώ.
Shopkeeper	Μάλιστα.
Customer	Πόσο κάνει;
Shopkeeper	Ογδόντα δραχμές.

Eating out

| Customer | Τό κατάλογο παρακαλώ. |
| Waiter | Αμέσως. Τί θά φάτε; |

And, finding your way around

Man	Συγγνώμη, πού είναι
	τό μουσείο παρακαλώ;
Girl	Τό δεύτερο στενό αριστερά καί τό
	πρώτο δεξιά.
Man	Ευχαριστώ.
Girl	Παρακαλώ.

Explanations

What would you like?

Τί θά πάρετε; 'what will you have?', **τί θέλετε;** 'what do you want?', and **παρακαλώ;** '(yes) please?' are expressions often used by waiters. However, listen out for two others beginning with **τί θά . . . ;** on the pattern of **τί θά πάρετε; –** they're **τί θά φάτε;** 'what will you eat?' and **τί θά πιείτε;** 'what will you drink?'

Bring us . . .

You'd normally say **φέρτε μας . . .** 'bring us . . . ' but you can also use **μάς φέρνετε . . . ;** If you were by yourself, it would be **φέρτε μου . . .** or **μού φέρνετε . . . ;** 'bring me'.

Exercises

1   Read these five orders for a quick snack out loud, and then match them with the five orders in English from the list below:

α   Ένα τόστ μέ ζαμπόν
β   Δύο τόστ μέ ζαμπόν καί τυρί
γ   Τρία σάντουϊτς μέ ζαμπόν καί τυρί
δ   Δύο τυρόπιττες
ε   Ένα σάντουϊτς μέ ζαμπόν, καί μία τυρόπιττα

a   Three ham and cheese sandwiches
b   Two cheese pies
c   A ham sandwich and a cheese pie
d   A toasted ham sandwich
e   Two toasted ham and cheese sandwiches

2   You're eating out with a friend. Work out your part of the conversation:

You   (call for the menu)............................
                  ....
Waiter   Αμέσως. Τί θά φάτε;

You	(one chicken and one veal cutlet) ....
	....
Waiter	Μάλιστα
You	(and a mixed salad please)...............
	....
Waiter	Τί θά πιείτε;
You	(half a kilo of wine . . .)...................
	....
Waiter	Αμέσως.
You	(. . . and water please)......................
	....
You	(call for the bill)
	....
	....
Waiter	Τετρακόσιες είκοσι δραχμές
You	(The bill comes to . . . . . drachmas. As you give him the money, say, 'Here you are, thank you')...............
	....
Waiter	Εγώ ευχαριστώ

3   In a taverna, the waiter offers you the choice of the following ορεκτικά. Have a go at reading them out loud. After that, you decide you'd like yoghurt and garlic, courgettes, and cheese pies. Tick the items you would order:

α   Τζατζίκι
β   Κολοκυθάκια
γ   Μελιτζάνες
δ   Χταποδάκι
ε   Τυροπιττάκια
ζ   Χωριάτικη σαλάτα

What else is on the list?...............................
....
....
....
....

4   You're in a snack bar with the family, who all
    want to try different things. Ask for:

i   A cheese pie.
ii   A toasted sandwich with ham.
iii A sandwich with ham and cheese.
iv   Two toasted sandwiches with cheese.
v   Three beers.

Worth knowing

Eating out

A ταβέρνα is normally open only in the evenings
and specialises in meat, and sometimes fish,
cooked over a charcoal grill, and a wide range of
hors d'oeuvres – ορεκτικά or μεζέδες. People go to a
ταβέρνα to spend the evening chatting over a slow
meal and one or two glasses of beer or wine. There
may also be singing and dancing. Usually, they will
order a number of hors d'oeuvres and spend some
time over those before proceeding to the main
dish. Sweets are limited – usually to fresh fruit. And
coffee is not usually served, since it is not a Greek
habit to drink coffee after a meal. People will either
sit on in the ταβέρνα after the meal, or perhaps go
on to a ζαχαροπλαστείο for an ice-cream or a cake.

An εστιατόριο is open throughout the day. Though
it, too, may have a charcoal grill (normally only
used in the evenings) it differs from the ταβέρνα in
having a large number of ready-cooked dishes.
Many εστιατόρια are particularly busy at lunch
times (2 pm-3 pm).

The ταβέρνα will frequently not have a menu (the
waiter will tell you what's on) though the εστιατόριο
probably will have one. In both it is quite common
for people to go into the kitchen to see what looks
good before they order.

Wine

You can order wine by the bottle – μπουκάλι – or the draught house wine by weight: ένα κιλό, μισόκιλο or ένα τέταρτο. A kilo is about a litre. For a single glass of wine, ask for ένα ποτήρι (water glass size) or ένα ποτηράκι (wine glass).

What's on the menu?

The menu in an εστιατόριο can seem quite complicated. Look under the heading ΕΝΤΡΑΔΕΣ for main dishes, where you'll find μοσχάρι (veal), χοιρινό (pork), αρνί or αρνάκι (lamb) and κοτόπουλο (chicken) – each with a variety of garnishes. Under ΨΗΤΑ you'll find roast dishes, and ΛΑΔΕΡΑ (dishes cooked in oil) and ΚΥΜΑΔΕΣ (dishes with mince meat) will include things like κεφτέδες (meat balls) and ντομάτες γεμιστές (stuffed tomatoes).

If you want freshly cooked food (available mainly in the evening) try the section headed ΤΗΣ ΩΡΑΣ (food cooked 'at the time').

Salads are listed under ΣΑΛΑΤΕΣ and sweets under ΓΛΥΚΑ. The most common dessert, however, is fresh fruit, found under ΦΡΟΥΤΑ.

The Greek habit is to eat much later than in England. The restaurants fill up at lunch time between 2 pm and 3 pm: and in the evening, 9 pm is an early time to start – a ταβέρνα will fill up between 10 pm and 11 pm.

Snacks

One common snack in Greece is σουβλάκι μέ πίττα, chunks of grilled meat and salad wrapped in pitta bread. And there are many snack-bars where you can buy a τυρόπιττα 'cheese pie', a σπανακόπιττα 'spinach pie', a κρεατόπιττα 'meat pie', or a μπουγάτσα 'pastry filled with custard'. There are also snack-bars where you can buy a toasted sandwich (τόστ) or a plain sandwich (σάντουιτς). Both have a wide variety of fillings.

Can you 'GET BY'?

Try these exercises when you've finished the course. The answers are on page 69.

1   Choose a suitable greeting from the list below for each of these situations:

i   You meet Mr Pappas at a dinner party in the evening
ii   You meet your friend Nikos by chance in a bookshop
iii You go into a travel agency in the middle of the morning
iv   You leave a group of friends at a taverna about midnight to go back to your hotel
v   You say goodbye to the hotel receptionist as you leave to catch your plane home

α   Καλημέρα σας
β   Καλησπέρα
γ   Γειά σου
δ   Αντίο σας
ε   Καληνύχτα σας

2
a   You meet your new colleague's wife for the first time. How do you say 'Hello, how are you?'

    ....

b   She says **καλά ευχαριστώ, εσείς;** How do you say 'Very well thank you'? ....

    ....

c   Now you meet her brother, who asks **Τί κάνετε;** How do you say 'I'm well thanks, how about you?' ....

    ....

d You meet an old friend on the boat to Samos.
   Say 'Hello, how are you?' ....
   ....
e He says μία χαρά, εσύ; How do you say you're
   well?...
f Another close friend meets you from the boat
   and asks τί κάνεις; How do you say, 'I'm fine,
   how are you?' ....
   ....

3 Read the following questions and requests out
loud, and then choose the situation in which you
might say them from the list below.

α Ένα σκέτο παρακαλώ
β Μήπως έχετε αυγά;
γ Μήπως έχετε δωμάτια;
δ Θέλω νά χαλάσω πενήντα λίρες
ε Πού είναι τό μουσείο παρακαλώ;
ζ Τί ώρα φεύγει τό καράβι;
η Γιά τό Σούνιο πάει αυτό;
θ Τό κατάλογο παρακαλώ;
ι Γιά ορεκτικά τί έχετε;
κ Μία τυρόπιττα παρακαλώ

i   In a hotel
ii   In the street
iii At the bus station
iv   At the ταβέρνα
v   In a snack-bar
vi   At a ζαχαροπλαστείο
vii At a grocer's
viii At a bank
ix   At a travel agency
x   In an εστιατόριο

4 You're in a ζαχαροπλαστείο and a group of
friends want you to show off your Greek and do all
the ordering. How do you ask for:
a a sweet coffee ....

b   an instant coffee with milk.................................
    ....
c   one tea with lemon...
d   two teas with milk ....
    ....
e   three beers ....
f   two medium coffees...

5   You're out shopping. How do you ask for these items:
a   half a kilo of ham ....
b   one kilo of tomatoes..
c   a dozen eggs ....
d   a bottle of retsina...
    ....
e   a map of Athens ....

6   You've just arrived in a small town, and you want to find a hotel and some other places nearby. How do you ask:
a   Is there a hotel nearby?......................................
    ....
b   Where is the museum? ....
    ....
c   Where is the bank?..
    ....
d   Is there a chemist's anywhere nearby? ....
    ....
e   Where is the baker's?..
    ....
f   Is there a kiosk nearby?......................................
    ....

7   Look at the following sets of directions. Pick out the key words, and note down the way you have to go (eg first right, second left):
α   Θά πάρετε τό πρῶτο στενό ἀριστερά, καί μετά θά
    στρίψετε στό πρῶτο δεξιά ....
    ....

β   Θά στρίψετε αριστερά στή γωνία, καί θά πάρετε
    τό τρίτο στενό δεξιά.......................................
    ....

γ   Τό δεύτερο στενό δεξιά, καί μετά τό τρίτο
    αριστερά...
    ....

δ   Θά πάτε ευθεία καί θά στρίψετε αριστερά στή
    γωνία ....

ε   Θά πάρετε τό πρώτο στενό αριστερά καί μετά τό
    τρίτο στενό αριστερά....................................
    ....

8   Read the following prices out loud and then
write down in figures how much they are:

α   Πενήντα πέντε ....
β   Ογδόντα τρείς..
γ   Εκατόν εξήντα μία...
δ   Πεντακόσιες εβδομήντα εννιά.........................
ε   Χίλιες διακόσιες...
ζ   Τρείς χιλιάδες τετρακόσιες σαράντα ....

9   You're planning your holiday excursions. How
do you ask:

a   What time does the boat to Rhodes (**γιά τή
    Ρόδο**) leave?...

b   What time does it arrive?................................

c   How much does it cost?..................................

d   What time does the bus to Sounio leave?..........
    ....

e   What time does it arrive?................................

f   How much does it cost?..................................

g   Where does it leave from?...............................
    ....

h   Does this go to Rhodes? ....
    ....

i   Does this go to Sounio?..................................
    ....

10 Choose a suitable answer for the following questions and requests:

i Τί δωμάτιο θέλετε;
α ένα μονόκλινο
β τής Αθήνας παρακαλώ
γ ένα ζεστό νές

ii Τί θά φάτε;
α μία μπύρα
β ένα σουβλάκι
γ τρείς καφέδες

iii Τί θέλετε;
α όχι, ευχαριστώ
β πολύ καλά ευχαριστώ
γ μισόκιλο ντομάτες

iv Τό όνομά σας;
α εντάξει
β Παππάς
γ ορίστε

v Τίποτ᾽άλλο;
α όχι, ευχαριστώ
β εδώ
γ καλημέρα σας

vi Τί θά πιείτε;
α μία μπριζόλα μοσχαρίσια
β μία χωριάτικη
γ μισόκιλο κρασί

vii Τό διαβατήριό σας;
α ορίστε
β Παππάς
γ τρείς

viii Πόσα θέλετε;
α νερό παρακαλώ
β ένα καφέ
γ δέκα

Reference section

Language

The Greek you hear on the cassettes is typical of that spoken in Athens and throughout most of Greece. Although there are local dialects in a few parts of Greece you will certainly be understood everywhere when you speak the Greek you've learned, and you should have few problems getting used to the local accent. This is also true of Cyprus, which has a particularly distinct dialect.

Pronunciation guide

Hardly any of the sounds in Greek present any difficulty for the English-speaker. In this guide you'll find the alphabet written out with the name of each letter and an indication as to its approximate pronunciation. In the right-hand column you'll find a number opposite each letter. This refers to a word which contains the sound in the list at the end of the alphabet section. Practise saying each word out loud, first using the English 'guide' and then looking at the Greek as you say it, to help you become familiar with the way Greek looks. You can hear all the words in the list on Cassette 2, after the end of unit 5.

In this way you'll soon become familiar with the Greek alphabet, and be able to read and speak all the Greek you need.

It is not important to try to acquire a 'perfect accent': the aim is to be understood. for this it *is* important that you stress the right part of the word – and in Greek each word has a stress-mark on it (see page 61).

The alphabet

Capital letter	Small letter	Name	Approx sound	Example number
A	α	*alfa*	c**a**t	1
B	β	*vita*	**v**oice	22
Γ	γ	*gama*	i ba**g** (soft 'g') ii **y**es (before 'e' and 'i')	9 23
Δ	δ	*thelta*	**th**is	29
E	ε	*epsilon*	t**e**n	4
Z	ζ	*zita*	**z**oo	13
H	η	*ita*	f**ee**t (clipped short)	20
Θ	θ	*thita*	**th**ick	8
I	ι	*yota*	f**ee**t (clipped short)	7
K	κ	*kapa*	**k**ing	1
Λ	λ	*lamtha*	**l**ong	18
M	μ	*mi*	**m**an	19
N	ν	*ni*	**n**ot	20
Ξ	ξ	*xi*	bo**x**	31
O	ο	*omikron*	t**au**t (clipped short)	10
Π	π	*pi*	**p**it	28
P	ρ	*ro*	**r**ed	2
Σ	σ, ⋆ς	*sigma*	**s**it	15/25
T	τ	*taf*	**t**op	23
Y	υ	*ipsilon*	f**ee**t (clipped short)	10
Φ	φ	*fi*	**f**at	32
X	χ	*khi*	i lo**ch** ii **h**ue (before 'e' and 'i')	27 26

⋆ς is used at the end of words

| Ψ | ψ | *psi* | la**ps**e | 7 |
| Ω | ω | *omega* | t**au**t (clipped short) | 27 |

Combinations of letters

	Approx sound	Example number
αι	t**e**n	26
ει	f**ee**t (clipped short)	15
οι	f**ee**t (clipped short)	16
αυ	i **af**ter	5
	ii **av**oid	6
ευ	i l**ef**t	27
	ii **ev**er	17
ου	m**oo**n	24
γγ	E**ng**land	21
γκ	**g**o	14
γχ	in**h**erent	33
μπ	i slu**mb**er	3
	ii **b**at	2
ντ	i be**nd**ing	11
	ii **d**og	25

Certain sounds can be written in more than one way: αι and ε have exactly the same sound. So do ο and ω. And η, ι, υ, ει and οι all represent the same sound.

Practice words

Don't worry about the meaning of the words at this stage (most of them occur in the early part of the course) – concentrate on how they sound and on relating the sound to the Greek letters.

1 καφέ kafé	12 κέντρο kéndro	23 γεμάτοι yemáti
2 μπύρα bíra	13 ζεστό zestó	24 μουσείο moosío
3 ζαμπόν zambón	14 γκαρσόν garsón	25 ντομάτες domátes
4 έξι éxi	15 κλειστό klistó	26 χαίρετε hérete
5 αυτό aftó	16 ανοιχτό anihtó	27 ευχαριστώ efharistó
6 αυγά avgá	17 φεύγει févgi	28 παρακαλώ parakaló
7 ψωμί psomí	18 μπουκάλι boukáli	29 δωμάτιο thomátio
8 θέλω thélo	19 λεμόνι lemóni	30 καλησπέρα kalispéra
9 γάλα gála	20 Αθήνα Athína	31 ξενοδοχείο xenothohío
10 γλυκό glikó	21 Αγγλία Anglía	32 λεωφορείο leoforío
11 πέντε pénde	22 βεβαίως vevéos	33 μέ συγχωρείτε me sinhoríte

---

Accents

Words written in small letters have an accent to
show which part is stressed. Under the system
recently introduced in Greece only one kind of
accent mark ´ is used. If you see words written
under the old system, which had three different
accent marks ´ ` ^, remember that all of them
simply indicate the part of the word to be stressed.
The two signs ᾿ ῾ at the beginning of some words
have no effect on the way the word is said.

εξήντα ένα **61**

Masculine, feminine and neuter

Greek names for things and people are divided into three groups: masculine, feminine and neuter. The word for 'the' is different for each group: for masculine words it's **o**, for feminine words it's **η**, and for neuter words it's **τό**: **o φούρνος** is masculine, **η ταβέρνα** is feminine, and **τό εστιατόριο** is neuter. In the word list, **o, η,** or **τό** is given with the word: try to remember the two together.

γιά τό ... γιά τή ... When you're asking for 'the (bus) for ...', it will be **γιά τή** with feminine places and **γιά τό** with masculine and neuter places. You'll sometimes hear **γιά τήν** and **γιά τόν** with feminine and masculine places (but never with neuter places) if the name of the place begins with a vowel, for example, **γιά τήν Αθήνα**.

'A' and 'an'

When you're ordering things, or asking for things, the word for 'a' or 'an' is **ένα** with masculine and neuter words – **ένα καφέ, ένα ούζο** – and **μία** with feminine words – **μία μπύρα**.

Plurals

When you're ordering more than one of anything, the ending of the word changes. The list opposite shows some of the more common changes (not all of them occur in this course). Some foreign words don't change at all: **τόστ** and **σάντουιτς** for example.

Masculine words will normally end in **ς** when you look them up in a dictionary. This is the form you use, for example, when you ask how much something costs – **πόσο κάνει ο καφές;** or **πόσο κάνει ο χάρτης;** When you want to order something, ask for something, say you want something and so on, you leave off this ς: eg **ένα καφέ παρακαλώ, θέλω ένα χάρτη.** These are the endings given in the table.

Masculine words

-ο	-ους	ένα σκέτο	δύο σκέτους
-η	-ες	ένα χάρτη	δύο χάρτες
-α	-ες	ένα άντρα	δύο άντρες
but note that it's		ένα καφέ	δύο καφέδες

Feminine words

-α	-ες	μία μπύρα	δύο μπύρες
-η	-ες	μία δραχμή	δύο δραχμές

Neuter words

-ο	-α	ένα δωμάτιο	δύο δωμάτια
-α	-ατα	ένα γράμμα	δύο γράμματα
-ι	-ια	ένα καράβι	δύο καράβια

Adjectives – describing words

If you're ordering things, or saying you want things, many common adjectives end in **-ο** if the word is masculine, **-η** if it's feminine and **-ο** if it's neuter (and change to **-ους, -ες, -α** if you're wanting more than one).

Numbers

0	μηδέν	10	δέκα		
1	ένα	11	έντεκα		
2	δύο	12	δώδεκα	20	είκοσι
3	τρία	13	δεκατρία	30	τριάντα
4	τέσσερα	14	δεκατέσσερα	40	σαράντα
5	πέντε	15	δεκαπέντε	50	πενήντα
6	έξι	16	δεκαέξι	60	εξήντα
7	εφτά	17	δεκαεφτά	70	εβδομήντα
8	οχτώ	18	δεκαοχτώ	80	ογδόντα
9	εννιά	19	δεκαεννιά	90	ενενήντα

100 εκατό		600 εξακόσια
200 διακόσια		700 εφτακόσια
300 τριακόσια		800 οχτακόσια
400 τετρακόσια		900 εννιακόσια
500 πεντακόσια		

1000 χίλια
2000 δύο χιλιάδες
3000 τρείς χιλιάδες
4000 τέσσερεις χιλιάδες
10,000 δέκα χιλιάδες
100,000 εκατό χιλιάδες

One is **μία** with feminine words, and **ένα** when you're ordering masculine or neuter things. Three and four are **τρία** and **τέσσερα** with neuter words, or when you're just counting, and **τρείς** and **τέσσερεις** with masculine and feminine words. Thirteen and fourteen – **δεκατρία** and **δεκατέσσερα** – also change in this way, as well as all other numbers ending in one, three or four.

The hundreds – **διακόσια, τριακόσια** etc – become **διακόσιες, τριακόσιες** and so on, with feminine words, and one thousand – **χίλια** – becomes **χίλιες**. Since **δραχμή** is a feminine word, prices are given in this form. Numbers are combined as follows (they are given in the feminine, as though they were prices):

24	είκοσι τέσσερεις
231	διακόσιες τριάντα μία
1,763	χίλιες εφτακόσιες εξήντα τρείς
13,845	δεκατρείς χιλιάδες οχτακόσιες σαράντα πέντε

100 – **εκατό** – is **εκατόν** when the following word begins with a vowel and so it's:

εκατό δεκαέξι (116)
but εκατόν είκοσι έξι (126)

Days of the week

Κυριακή	*Sunday*
Δευτέρα	*Monday*
Τρίτη	*Tuesday*
Τετάρτη	*Wednesday*
Πέμπτη	*Thursday*
Παρασκευή	*Friday*
Σάββατο	*Saturday*

Months of the year

You will hear two forms of these:

Γεννάρης	Ιανουάριος	*January*
Φλεβάρης	Φεβρουάριος	*February*
Μάρτης	Μάρτιος	*March*
Απρίλης	Απρίλιος	*April*
Μάης	Μάϊος	*May*
Ιούνης	Ιούνιος	*June*
Ιούλης	Ιούλιος	*July*
Αύγουστος	Αύγουστος	*August*
Σεπτέμβρης	Σεπτέμβριος	*September*
Οχτώβρης	Οκτώβριος	*October*
Νοέμβρης	Νοέμβριος	*November*
Δεκέμβρης	Δεκέμβριος	*December*

Sign language

The following signs are very common, and you will find it useful to be able to recognise them:

ΕΙΣΟΔΟΣ	**ΕΞΟΔΟΣ**
ENTRANCE	EXIT
ΑΝΟΙΚΤΟΝ	**ΚΛΕΙΣΤΟΝ**
OPEN	CLOSED
ΩΘΗΣΑΤΕ	**ΣΥΡΑΤΕ**
PUSH	PULL

ΑΠΑΓΟΡΕΥΕΤΑΙ	ΕΠΙΤΡΕΠΕΤΑΙ
IT IS FORBIDDEN	IT IS ALLOWED

In the lift

ΣΤΑΣΙΣ	STOP
ΚΙΝΔΥΝΟΣ	DANGER
3 ος	3rd floor
2 ος	2nd floor
1 ος	1st floor
ΗΜ=ΗΜΙΟΡΟΦΟΣ	MEZZANINE FLOOR
ΙΣ=ΙΣΟΓΕΙΟΝ	GROUND FLOOR
ΥΠΟΓ=ΥΠΟΓΕΙΟΝ	BASEMENT

Useful addresses

Greek National Tourist Office

195-197 Regent Street   Odos Amerikis 2
London W1R 8DR   Athens
(Tel: 01-734 5997)   (Tel: 322-3111)

Cyprus Tourism Organisation

213 Regent Street   Odos Th. Theodotou 18
London W1R 8DA   PO Box 4535
(Tel: 01-734 9822)   Nikosia
                            (Tel: 021 43374)

Olympic Airways

141 New Bond Street
London W1
(Tel: 01-493 4262)

Odos Othonos 6
Sindagma Square
Athens
(Tel: 929-2444)
(Telephone
 reservations:
 923-2323)

Leoforos Singrou 96
Athens
(Tel: 92921)

Odos Sindagmatos 2
PO Box 46
Limassol
(Tel: 051 62145/6)

Embassies and Consulates

United Kingdom
Odos Ploutarchou 1
Athens
(Tel: 723-6211/9)

*British High
  Commission*
Odos Alexander Pallis
PO Box 1978
Nikosia
(Tel: 021 73131)

Eire
Leoforos Vas.
  Konstantinou 7
Athens
(Tel: 723-2771/2)

Main Tourist Police Office

Leoforos Singrou 7
Athens
(Tel: 923-9224)

Key to exercises

Chapter 1

1 i α, ii β, iii β, iv γ, v δ
2 a ε, b δ, c ζ, d β

3 α, β, γ, γ
4 α, α, β, γ, α

Chapter 2

1 a γ, b β, c γ, d α, e γ
2 b, β, c, β, α, b
3 i   μισόκιλο ντομάτες
    ii ένα τέταρτο ζαμπόν
    iii έξι αυγά
    iv ένα μπουκάλι ρετσίνα
4 i 40 drachmas, ii 30, iii 30, iv 85: total 185

Chapter 3

1 Γειά σας (Χαίρετε)
Μήπως έχετε δωμάτια;
Ένα μονόκλινο παρακαλώ
Ναί (Μάλιστα)
Τέσσερεις
Πόσο κάνει;
Εντάξει
Ορίστε

2 α i, β ii, γ iii, δ iv, ε v

3 a διακόσια πέντε
b τριακόσια πέντε
c τριακόσια δέκα
d τετρακόσια δέκα
e πεντακόσια εφτά

4 a πενήντα λίρες
b είκοσι λίρες
c εκατό λίρες
d είκοσι πέντε λίρες
e σαράντα λίρες

Chapter 4

1 α ii, β v, γ iii

2 i Υπάρχει ταχυδρομείο εδώ κοντά;
ii Υπάρχει τράπεζα εδώ κοντά;
iii Υπάρχει περίπτερο εδώ κοντά;
iv Υπάρχει φαρμακείο εδώ κοντά;
v Υπάρχει ζαχαροπλαστείο εδώ κοντά;
vi Υπάρχει ταβέρνα εδώ κοντά;

3 α iii, β ii, γ v, δ iv, ε i, ζ vi

4 Τί ώρα φεύγει τό καράβι γιά τή Ρόδο;
Τί ώρα φτάνει;
Εντάξει. Δύο παρακαλώ
Πόσο κάνουνε;
Ορίστε

Chapter 5

1 α d, β e, γ a, δ b, ε c

2 Τό κατάλογο παρακαλώ
Ένα κοτόπουλο καί μία μπριζόλα μοσχαρίσια
Καί μία χωριάτικη παρακαλώ
Μισόκιλο κρασί
Καί νερό παρακαλώ
Τό λογαριασμό παρακαλώ (420 drs)
Ορίστε. Ευχαριστώ

3 α, β, ε,
γ aubergines
δ octopus
ζ mixed salad

4 i μία τυρόπιττα
ii ένα τόστ μέ ζαμπόν
iii ένα σάντουιτς μέ ζαμπόν καί τυρί
iv δύο τόστ μέ τυρί
v τρείς μπύρες

Test

1 i β, ii γ, iii α, iv ε, v δ

2 a Γειά σας (Χαίρετε). Τί κάνετε;
   b Πολύ καλά ευχαριστώ
   c Καλά ευχαριστώ. Εσείς;
   d Γειά σου. Τί κάνεις;
   e Καλά
   f Μιά χαρά. Εσύ;

3 α vi, β vii, γ i, δ viii, ε ii
   ζ ix, η iii, θ x, ι iv, κ v

4 a ένα γλυκό
   b ένα νές μέ γάλα
   c ένα τσάι μέ λεμόνι
   d δύο τσάϊα μέ γάλα
   e τρείς μπύρες
   f δύο μέτριους

5 a μισόκιλο ζαμπόν
   b ένα κιλό ντομάτες
   c δώδεκα αυγά
   d ένα μπουκάλι ρετσίνα
   e ένα χάρτη τής Αθήνας

6 a Υπάρχει ξενοδοχείο εδώ κοντά;
   b Πού είναι τό μουσείο;
   c Πού είναι η τράπεζα;
   d Υπάρχει φαρμακείο εδώ κοντά;
   e Πού είναι ο φούρνος;
   f Υπάρχει περίπτερο εδώ κοντά;

7 α first left, first right
   β left at corner, third right.
   γ second right, third left
   δ straight on, left at corner
   ε first left, third left.

8 α 55, β 83, γ 161, δ 579, ε 1200, ζ 3,440

9 a Τί ώρα φεύγει τό καράβι γιά τή Ρόδο;
   b Τί ώρα φτάνει;
   c Πόσο κάνει;
   d Τί ώρα φεύγει τό λεωφορείο γιά τό Σούνιο;
   e Τί ώρα φτάνει;
   f Πόσο κάνει;
   g Από πού φεύγει;
   h Γιά τή Ρόδο πάει αυτό;
   i Γιά τό Σούνιο πάει αυτό;

10 i α, ii β, iii γ, iv β, v α, vi γ, vii α, viii γ

ΑΒΓΔΕΖΗΘΙΚΛΜΝΞΟΠΡΣΤΥΦΧΨΩ
αβγδεζηθικλμνξοπρστυφχψω

Word list

This word list gives the meaning of each word and also a pronunciation guide in English letters. It includes all the words used in this book. Adjectives are given in the form in which they appear in the course: this sometimes means they are given more than once. Shop signs etc. that appear in capital letters in the book are listed here in capital letters, and some words appear both with capitals and with small letters.

The Greek alphabet is printed across the top of each page so that you can refer to it when checking words.

Α α

η Αγγλία *England* (Anglía)
η Αγγλίδα *Englishwoman* (Anglítha)
  Αγγλικά *English (language)* (Angliká)
ο 'Άγγλος *Englishman* ('Anglos)
τό αεροπλάνο *plane* (aëropláno)
η Αθήνα *Athens* (Athína)
  ΑΛΛΑΝΤΙΚΑ *SAUSAGE SHOP* (allandiká)
  αμέσως *right away* (amésos)
η Αμερικανίδα *American woman* (Amerikanítha)
  Αμερικάνικα *American (language)* (Amerikánika)
  αμερικάνικο *American (coffee)* (amerikániko)
ο Αμερικάνος *American man* (Amerikános)
η Αμερική *America* (Amerikí)
  ΑΝΔΡΩΝ *MEN'S TOILETS* (andrón)
  ΑΝΟΙΚΤΟΝ *OPEN* (aniktón)
η άνοιξη *spring* (ánixi)
  ανοιχτό *open* (anihtó)
  αντίο (σας) *goodbye* (adío(sas))

ο άντρας *man* (ándras)
  ΑΠΑΓΟΡΕΥΕΤΑΙ *IT IS FORBIDDEN* (apagorévete)
  απλή *ordinary (petrol)* (aplí)
  από *from* (apó)
τό απόγευμα *late afternoon/ early evening* (apóyevma)
  ΑΠΟΧΩΡΗΤΗΡΙΑ *TOILETS* (apohoritíria)
ο Απρίλης *April* (Aprílis)
ο Απρίλιος *April* (Aprílios)
  αργά *slowly* (argá)
ο αριθμός *number* (arithmós)
  αριστερά *left* (aristerá)
τό αρνάκι *lamb* (arnáki)
τό αρνί *mutton* (arní)
  ΑΡΤΟΠΟΙΕΙΟΝ *BAKER'S* (artopiíon)
  ΑΡΤΟΠΩΛΕΙΟΝ *BAKER'S* (artopolíon)
η αστυνομία *police* (astinomía)
τό αυγό *egg* (avgó)
ο Αύγουστος *August* (ávgoostos)
  αύριο *tomorrow* (ávrio)
  αυτό *this, that* (aftó)

Α Β Γ Δ Ε Ζ Η Θ Ι Κ Λ Μ Ν Ξ Ο Π Ρ Σ Τ Υ Φ Χ Ψ Ω
α β γ δ ε ζ η θ ι κ λ μ ν ξ ο π ρ σ τ υ φ χ ψ ω

Β β

βέβαια *certainly, of course* (vévea)
βεβαίως *certainly, of course* (vevéos)
η βενζίνη *petrol* (venzíni)
η βοήθεια *help* (voíthia)
τό βράδυ *evening* (vráthi)

Γ γ

τό γάλα *milk* (gála)
η Γαλλία *France* (Gallía)
η Γαλλίδα *Frenchwoman* (Gallítha)
Γαλλικά *French (language)* (Gallika)
γαλλικό *French (coffee)* (gallikó)
o Γάλλος *Frenchman* (Gállos)
γειά σας *hello or goodbye (formal)* (yásas)
γειά σου *hello or goodbye (informal)* (yásoo)
γεμάτοι *full (at the hotel)* (yemáti)
γεμιστές *stuffed (tomatoes)* (yemistés)
o Γεννάρης *January* (Yennáris)
η Γερμανία *Germany* (Yermanía)
η Γερμανίδα *German woman* (Yermanítha)
Γερμανικά *German (language)* (Yermaniká)
o Γερμανός *German man* (Yermanós)
γιά *for, to* (ya)
o γιατρός *doctor* (yatrós)
Γιώργος *(man's name)* (Yórgos)
γκαρσόν! *waiter!* (garsón)
ΓΛΥΚΑ *SWEETS (on menu)* (gliká)

γλυκό *sweet (coffee)* (glikó)
τό γράμμα *letter* (grámma)
τό γραμματόσημο *stamp* (grammatósimo)
η γρανίτα *sorbet* (graníta)
ΓΥΝΑΙΚΩΝ *WOMEN'S TOILETS* (yinekón)
η γωνία *corner* (gonía)

Δ δ

δέκα *ten* (théka)
δεκαέξι *sixteen* (thekaéxi)
δεκαεφτά *seventeen* (thekaeftá)
δεκαεννιά *nineteen* (thekaenniá)
δεκαοχτώ *eighteen* (thekaohtó)
δεκαπέντε *fifteen* (thekapénde)
τό δεκάρικο *ten-drachma piece* (thekáriko)
δεκατέσσερα *fourteen (n)* (thekatéssera)
δεκατέσσερεις *fourteen (m, f)* (thekatésseris)
δεκατρείς *thirteen (m, f)* (thekatrís)
δεκατρία *thirteen (n)* (thekatría)
o Δεκέμβρης *December* (Thekémvris)
o Δεκέμβριος *December* (Thekémvrios)
δέν *not* (then)
δεξιά *right (direction)* (thexiá)
δεσποινίς *Miss* (thespinís)
η Δευτέρα *Monday* (Theftéra)
δεύτερη *second (class)* (théfteri)
δεύτερο *second (street, floor)* (théftero)

ΑΒΓΔΕΖΗΘΙΚΛΜΝΞΟΠΡΣΤΥΦΧΨΩ
αβγδεζηθικλμνξοπρστυφχψω

τό διαβατήριο *passport*
(thiavatírio)
διακόσια *two hundred*
(thiakósia)
διακόσιες *two hundred*
(drachmas) (thiakósies)
τό δίκλινο *double room*
(thíklino)
διπλό *double (bed)* (thipló)
τό δίφραγκο *two-drachma*
piece (thífrango)
η δραχμή *drachma* (thrahmí)
δύο *two* (thío)
δυόμιση *half past two*
(thiómisi)
δυστυχώς *unfortunately*
(thistihós)
δώδεκα *twelve* (thótheka)
δωδεκάμιση *half past*
twelve (thothekámisi)
τό δωμάτιο *room* (thomátio)

Ε ε

η εβδομάδα *week*
(evthomátha)
εβδομήντα *seventy*
(evthomínda)
εγώ *I* (egó)
εδώ *here* (ethó)
τό εικοσάρικο *twenty-*
drachma piece (ikosáriko)
είκοσι *twenty* (íkosi)
είμαστε *we are* (ímaste)
είναι *is* (íne)
ΕΙΣΟΔΟΣ *ENTRANCE*
(ísothos)
ΕΙΣΠΡΑΚΤΟΡΑ
CONDUCTOR (see
ΧΩΡΙΣ*)* (ispráktora)
εκατό *one hundred* (ekató)
η Ελλάδα *Greece* (Ellátha)
ο Έλληνας *Greek man*
('Ellinas)
η Ελληνίδα *Greek woman*
(Ellinítha)

Ελληνικά *Greek (language)*
(Elliniká)
ΕΛΠΑ *Greek Motoring*
Organisation (élpa)
ένα *a, an, one* (éna)
ενενήντα *ninety* (enenínda)
εννέα *nine* (ennéa)
εννιά *nine* (enniá)
εννιακόσια *nine hundred*
(enniakósia)
εννιακόσιες *nine hundred*
(drachmas) (enniakósies)
εννιάμιση *half past nine*
(enniámisi)
εντάξει *okay* (endáxi)
έντεκα *eleven* (éndeka)
εντεκάμιση *half past eleven*
(endekámisi)
ΕΝΤΡΑΔΕΣ *MAIN DISHES*
(heading on menu)
(entráthes)
εξακόσια *six hundred*
(exakósia)
εξακόσιες *six hundred*
(drachmas) (exakósies)
εξήντα *sixty* (exínda)
έξι *six* (éxi)
εξίμιση *half past six*
(exímisi)
ΕΞΟΔΟΣ *EXIT* (éxothos)
ΕΠΙΤΡΕΠΕΤΑΙ *IT IS*
ALLOWED (epitrépete)
επτά *seven* (eptá)
επτάμιση *half past seven*
(eptámisi)
εσείς *you (formal and*
plural) (esís)
τό εσπρέσσο *espresso*
(esprésso)
τό εστιατόριο *restaurant*
(estiatório)
ΕΣΤΙΑΤΟΡΙΟΝ
RESTAURANT
(estiatórion)
εσύ *you (informal and*

ΑΒΓΔΕΖΗΘΙΚΛΜΝΞΟΠΡΣΤΥΦΧΨΩ
αβγδεζηθικλμνξοπρστυφχψω

singular) esí
ευθεία *straight on* (efthía)
ευχαριστώ *thank you*
(efharistó)
ευχαρίστως *with pleasure*
(efharístos)
εφτά *seven* (eftá)
εφτακόσια *seven hundred*
(eftakósia)
εφτακόσιες *seven hundred
(drachmas)* (eftakósies)
εφτάμιση *half past seven*
(eftámisi)
έχασα . . . *I've lost . . .*
(éhasa)
έχετε *you have, do you
have . . .* (éhete)
έχουμε *we have* (éhoome)
έχω *I have* (ého)

Ζ ζ
τό ζαμπόν *ham* (zambón)
τό ζαχαροπλαστείο *patisserie*
(zaharoplastío)
ζεστό *hot (ένα ζεστό* νες μέ
γαλα *a hot instant coffee
with milk)* (zestó)

Η η
η *the (with f words)* (i)
ή *or* (í)
ο ηλεκτρικός *Athens
underground* (ilektrikós)
ΗΜΙΟΡΟΦΟΣ
MEZZANINE FLOOR
(imiórofos)
Ηνωμένες Πολιτείες *United
States* (Inoménes
Politíes)

Θ θ
θά *indicates 'will' 'shall' eg*
τί θά πάρετε; (tha)
θέλετε *you want, do you*

want? (thélete)
θέλω *I want* (thélo)

Ι ι
ο Ιανουάριος *January*
(Yanwários)
ο Ιούλης *July* (Yoólis)
ο Ιούλιος *July* (Yoólios)
ο Ιούνης *June* (Yoónis)
ο Ιούνιος *June* (Yoónios)
η Ιρλανδέζα *Irish woman*
(Irlanthéza)
η Ιρλανδία *Ireland* (Irlanthía)
ο Ιρλανδός *Irish man*
(Irlanthós)
ίσια *straight on* (ísia)
ΙΣΟΓΕΙΟΝ *GROUND
FLOOR* (isóyion)
η Ισπανία *Spain* (Ispanía)
η Ισπανίδα *Spanish woman*
(Ispanítha)
Ισπανικά *Spanish
(language)* (Ispaniká)
ο Ισπανός *Spanish man*
(Ispanós)
η Ιταλία *Italy* (Italía)
η Ιταλίδα *Italian woman*
(Italítha)
Ιταλικά *Italian (language)*
(Italiká)
υ Ιταλός *Italian man* (Italós)

Κ κ
καθήστε *take a seat*
(kathíste)
καί *and* (ke)
καλά *well* (kalá)
καλημέρα *good morning,
good day* (kaliméra)
καληνύχτα *good night*
(kaliníhta)
καλησπέρα *good evening*
(kalispéra)
τό καλοκαίρι *summer*
(kalokéri)

Α Β Γ Δ Ε Ζ Η Θ Ι Κ Λ Μ Ν Ξ Ο Π Ρ Σ Τ Υ Φ Χ Ψ Ω
α β γ δ ε ζ η θ ι κ λ μ ν ξ ο π ρ σ τ υ φ χ ψ ω

κάνει *(πόσο κάνει; how much does it cost?)* (káni)

κάνεις *(τί κάνεις; how are you?) (informal)* (kánis)

κάνετε *(τί κάνετε; how are you?) (formal)* (kánete)

κάνουν/κάνουνε *(πόσο κάνουνε; how much do they cost?)* (kánoon/kánoone)

τό καπουτσίνο *capuccino* (kapootsíno)

τό καράβι *boat* (karávi)

τό κασέρι *kind of cheese* (kaséri)

δέν κατάλαβα *I don't understand* (then katálava)

ο κατάλογος *menu, list* (katálogos)

τό κατοστάρικο *hundred-drachma note* (katostáriko)

τό καφενείο *cafe* (kafenío)

ο καφές *coffee* (kafés)

τό κέντρο *centre* (kéndro)

κεφτέδες *meat balls* (keftéthes)

κι = καί *(κι εγώ ευχαριστώ thank you)*

τό κιλό *kilo* (kiló)

ΚΙΝΔΥΝΟΣ *DANGER* (kínthinos)

κλείσει *(έχω κλείσει I've reserved)* (klísi)

κλειστό *closed* (klistó)

ΚΛΕΙΣΤΟΝ *CLOSED* (klistón)

κολοκυθάκια *courgettes* (kolokithákia)

τό κονιάκ *brandy* (konyák)

κοντά *near, nearby* (kondá)

τό κοτόπουλο *chicken* (kotópoolo)

τό κρασί *wine* (krasí)

η κρεατόπιττα *meat pie* (kreatópitta)

ΚΡΕΟΠΩΛΕΙΟΝ *BUTCHER'S* (kreopolíon)

τό κρεββάτι *bed* (krevváti)

κρέμα *plain ice cream* (kréma)

ΚΥΜΑΔΕΣ *DISHES WITH MINCE (on menu)* (kimáthes)

ο κυμάς *mince meat* (kimás)

η κυρία *Mrs* (kiría)

η Κυριακή *Sunday* (Kiriakí)

κύριε *Mr (when speaking directly to someone)* (kírie)

ο κύριος *Mr* (kírios)

Λ λ

ΛΑΔΕΡΑ *COOKED WITH OIL (on menu)* (latherá)

η λεμονάδα *lemonade* (lemonátha)

τό λεμόνι *lemon* (lemóni)

τό λεπτό i *minute* ii *1/100th of a drachma* (leptó)

τό λεωφορείο *bus* (leoforío)

η λίρα *pound* (líra)

ο λογαριασμός *bill* (logariasmós)

τό λουκάνικο *sausage* (lookániko)

Μ μ

μαζί *(μαζί σας with you)* (mazí)

μάλιστα *certainly, yes* (málista)

ο Μάρτης *March* (Mártis)

ο Μάρτιος *March* (Mártios)

μέ *with* (me)

μέ συγχωρείτε *excuse me* (me sinhoríte)

μεζέδες *hors d'oeuvres* (mezéthes)

ΑΒΓΔΕΖΗΘΙΚΛΜΝΞΟΠΡΣΤΥΦΧΨΩ
αβγδεζηθικλμνξοπρστυφχψω

μεθαύριο *the day after tomorrow* (methávrio)
μείνετε *(πόσο θά μείνετε; how long are you staying?)* (mínete)
μελιτζάνες *aubergines* (melitzánes)
η μέρα *day* (méra)
μερικούς *some (hors d'oeuvres)* (merikoós)
τό μεσημέρι *the early afternoon* (mesiméri)
μετά *afterwards, next* (metá)
μέτριο *medium (coffee)* (métrio)
μεγάλη *large (beer)* (megáli)
μηδέν *zero* (mithén)
μήπως *(μήπως έχετε . . . ; do you have any . . . ?)* (mípos)
μία *a, an, one* (mía)
μιά χαρά *fine* (myá hará)
μιάμιση *half past one* (miámisi)
μικρή *small (beer)* (mikrí)
μιλάτε *do you speak? you speak* (miláte)
μισή *half (hour)* (misí)
τό μισόκιλο *half a kilo* (misókilo)
τό μονόκλινο *single room* (monóklino)
MONON *ONLY* (mónon)
τό μοσχάρι *veal* (moshári)
μοσχαρίσια *veal (cutlet)* (mosharísia)
ο μπακλαβάς *cake with nuts and honey* (baklavás)
τό μπάνιο *bath* (bánio)
τό μπόν φιλέ *steak* (bon filé)
η μπουγάτσα *kind of pastry* (boogátsa)
τό μπουκάλι *bottle* (bookáli)

η μπριζόλα *cutlet* (brizóla)
η μπύρα *beer* (bíra)
ΜΠΥΡΑΡΙΑ *CAFE SERVING BEER AND SNACKS* (biraría)

N ν
νά *(θέλω νά . . . I want to . . .)* (na)
ναί *yes* (ne)
τό νερό *water* (neró)
τό νές *instant coffee* (nes)
ο Νοέμβρης *November* (Noémvris)
ο Νοέμβριος *November* (Noémvrios)
τό ντούς *shower* (doós)
η νύχτα *night* (níhta)

Ξ ξ
τό ξενοδοχείο *hotel* (xenothohío)

O o
ο *the (with m words)* (o)
ογδόντα *eighty* (ogthónda)
η οδός *street* (othós)
ο Οκτώβριος *October* (Októvrios)
τό όνομα *name (τό όνομά σας παρακαλώ your name please)* (ónoma)
ορεκτικά *hors d'oeuvres* (orektiká)
ορίστε i *here you are* ii *yes, what is it?* (oríste)
ο όροφος *floor (1st 2nd etc)* (órofos)
ο ΟΣΕ *the railway company* (osé)
ο ΟΤΕ *Greek telecommunications service* (oté)
η Ουαλλέζα *Welsh woman* (Wallésa)

ΑΒΓΔΕΖΗΘΙΚΛΜΝΞΟΠΡΣΤΥΦΧΨΩ
αβγδεζηθικλμνξοπρστυφχψω

η Ουαλλία *Wales* (Wallía)
ο Ουαλλός *Welsh man* (Wallós)
τό ούζο *ouzo* (oózo)
όχι *no* (óhi)
οχτακόσια *eight hundred* (ohtakósia)
οχτακόσιες *eight hundred (drachmas)* (ohtakósies)
οχτώ *eight* (ohtó)
ο Οχτώβρης *October* (Ohtóvris)
οχτώμιση *half past eight* (ohtómisi)

Π π

τό παγωτό *ice cream* (pagotó)
πάει *goes* (pái)
ΠΑΝΤΟΠΩΛΕΙΟΝ *GROCER'S* (pandopolíon)
παρακαλώ *please, don't mention it* (parakaló)
η Παρασκευή *Friday* (Paraskeví)
πάρετε *have, take* (τί θά πάρετε; what will you have? θά τή πάρετε μαζί σας; will you take it with you?) (párete)
παρφέ *mixed ice cream* (parfé)
η πάστα *cake* (pásta)
η πατάτα *potato* (patáta)
η Πέμπτη *Thursday* (Pémpti)
πέμπτο *fifth (floor)* (pémpto)
πενήντα *fifty* (penínda)
τό πενηνταράκι *half-drachma piece* (penindaráki)
τό πενηντάρικο *fifty-drachma note, or piece* (penindáriko)
τό πεντακοσάρικο *five-hundred drachma note* (pendakosáriko)

πεντακόσια *five hundred* (pendakósia)
πεντακόσιες *five hundred (drachmas)* (pendakósies)
πέντε *five* (pénde)
πεντέμιση *half past five* (pendémisi)
περίπου *about, roughly* (perípoo)
τό περίπτερο *kiosk* (períptero)
πέρσι *last year* (pérsi)
πιείτε (τί θά πιείτε; *what will you drink?*) (pyíte)
πιό *more* (pyó)
η πιτσαρία *pizzeria* (pitsaría)
η πλατεία *square (eg* Πλατεία Αιγύπτου *Egypt Square)* (platía)
πολύ *very, much* (polí)
η πορτοκαλάδα *orangeade* (portokalátha)
τό πορτοκάλι *orange* (portokáli)
πόσα *how many* (pósa)
πόσες *how many* (póses)
πόσο *how much* (póso)
πόσους *how many* (pósoos)
τό ποτηράκι *wine glass* (potiráki)
τό ποτήρι *water glass* (potíri)
πού *where* (poó)
πρόσεξε *look out* (prósexe)
προσοχή *be careful* (prosohí)
προχτές *the day before yesterday* (prohtés)
τό πρωί *morning* (proí)
πρώτη *first (class)* (próti)
πρώτο *first (street, floor)* (próto)
πώς *yes* (pos)

Ρ ρ

η ρετσίνα *resinated wine*

ΑΒΓΔΕΖΗΘΙΚΛΜΝΞΟΠΡΣΤΥΦΧΨΩ
αβγδεζηθικλμνξοπρστυφχψω

(retsína)
η Ρωσσία *Russia* (Rossía)
η Ρωσσίδα *Russian woman* (Rossítha)
Ρωσσικά *Russian (language)* (Rossiká)
ο Ρώσσος *Russian man* (Rossos)

Σ σ (ς)
τό Σάββατο *Saturday* (Sávvato)
η σαλάτα *salad* (saláta)
ΣΑΛΑΤΕΣ *SALADS (heading on menu)* (salátes)
τό σάντουιτς *sandwich*
σαράντα *forty* (saránda)
σας *your (also added to* καλημέρα *etc to make them more formal)* (sas)
σέ *in, at, to* (se)
ο Σεπτέμβρης *September* (Septémvris)
ο Σεπτέμβριος *September* (Septémvrios)
σήμερα *today* (símera)
σικάγο *kind of ice cream* (sikágo)
σκέτο *without (coffee without sugar)* (skéto)
η Σκωτία *Scotland* (Skotía)
η Σκωτσέζα *Scotswoman* (Skotséza)
ο Σκωτσέζος *Scotsman* (Skotsézos)
ΣΝΑΚ ΜΠΑΡ *SNACK BAR* (snack bar)
σοκολάτα *chocolate (also chocolate ice cream)* (sokoláta)
τό σουβλάκι *meat grilled on a skewer* (soovláki)
σούπερ *super (petrol)*

(soóper)
ΣΟΥΠΕΡΜΑΡΚΕΤ *SUPERMARKET* (soopermárket)
η σπανακόπιττα *spinach pie* (spanakópitta)
ΣΤΑΣΙΣ i *STOP (in lift)* ii *BUS STOP* (stásis)
τό στενό *side street* (stenó)
στρίψετε *(θά στρίψετε . . . you turn . . .)* (strípsete)
συγγνώμη *excuse me* (signómi)
μέ συγχωρείτε *excuse me* (me sinhoríte)
ΣΥΝΑΛΛΑΓΜΑ *EXCHANGE* (sinállagma)
τό Σύνταγμα *Sindagma Square* (Síndagma)
ΣΥΡΑΤΕ *PULL* (sírate)

Τ τ
η ταβέρνα *taverna* (tavérna)
τό τάβλι *backgammon* (távli)
τό τάληρο *five-drachma piece* (táliro)
ΤΑΜΕΙΟΝ *CASH DESK* (tamíon)
τό ταχυδρομείο *post office* (tahithromío)
ΤΑΧΥΔΡΟΜΕΙΟΝ *POST OFFICE* (tahithromíon)
τέσσερα *four (n)* (téssera)
τέσσερεις *four (m,f)* (tésseris)
τεσσερεισήμιση *half past four* (tesserisímisi)
η Τετάρτη *Wednesday* (Tetárti)
τό τέταρτο i *quarter of a kilo* ii *quarter of an hour* (tétarto)
τέταρτο *fourth (floor, street)* (tétarto)

ΑΒΓΔΕΖΗΘΙΚΛΜΝΞΟΠΡΣΤΥΦΧΨΩ
αβγδεζηθικλμνξοπρστυφχψω

τετρακόσια *four hundred*
  (tetrakósia)
τετρακόσιες *four hundred*
  (drachmas) (tetrakósies)
τό τζατζίκι *yoghurt and*
  garlic salad (tzatzíki)
τό τηλέφωνο *telephone*
  (tiléfono)
  ΤΗΛΕΦΩΝΟΝ
  TELEPHONE (tiléfonon)
  ΤΗΣ ΩΡΑΣ *FRESHLY*
  COOKED DISHES
  (heading on menu)
  (tis óras)
  τί *what* (ti)
  τίποτ 'άλλο; *anything*
  else? (típot´állo)
τό *the (with n words)* (tó)
τό τόστ *toasted sandwich*
  (tóst)
  τουριστική *tourist (class)*
  (tooristikí)
  ΤΟΥΡΙΣΤΙΚΗ
  ΑΣΤΥΝΟΜΙΑ *TOURIST*
  POLICE
  (tooristikí astinomía)
τό τραίνο *train* (tréno)
η τράπεζα *bank* (trápeza)
  τρείς *three (m,f)* (trís)
  τρεισήμιση *half past three*
  (trisímisi)
  τρία *three (n)* (tría)
  τριακόσια *three hundred*
  (triakósia)
  τριακόσιες *three hundred*
  (drachmas) (triakósies)
  τριάντα *thirty* (triánda)
  τριάντα πέντε *thirty five*
  (triánda pénde)
τό τρίκλινο *room with three*
  beds (tríklino)
η Τρίτη *Tuesday* (Tríti)
  τρίτη *third (class)* (tríti)
  τρίτο *third (street, floor)*
  (tríto)

τό τσάϊ *tea* (tsáï)
τό τυρί *cheese* (tirí)
η τυρόπιττα *cheese pie*
  (tirópitta)
  τυροπιττάκια *small cheese*
  pies (tiropittákia)

Υ υ
  υπάρχει *is there?, there is*
  (ipárhi)
  ΥΠΕΡΑΓΟΡΑ
  SUPERMARKET
  (iperagorá)
  ΥΠΟΓΕΙΟΝ *BASEMENT*
  (ipóyion)
  υπογράψτε *sign (your*
  name) (ipográpste)

Φ φ
τό φαρμακείο *chemist's*
  (farmakío)
  ΦΑΡΜΑΚΕΙΟΝ
  CHEMIST'S (farmakíon)
  φάτε *(τί θά φάτε; what will*
  you eat?) (fáte)
ο Φεβρουάριος *February*
  (Fevrooários)
  φέρνετε *(μάς/μού*
  φέρνετε . . .;) bring
  us/me . . . (férnete)
  φέρτε *(φέρτε μας/μου . . .*
  bring us/me . . .) (férte)
η φέτα *goat's milk cheese*
  (féta)
  φέτος *this year* (fétos)
  φεύγει *leaves* (févgi)
τό φθινόπωρο *autumn*
  (fthinóporo)
ο Φλεβάρης *February*
  (Fleváris)
ο φούρνος *baker's* (foórnos)
τό φράγκο *one-drachma*
  piece (frángo)
  φραπέ *iced coffee* (frapé)
τό φρούτο *fruit* (froóto)
  ΦΡΟΥΤΑ *FRUIT (heading*

ΑΒΓΔΕΖΗΘΙΚΛΜΝΞΟΠΡΣΤΥΦΧΨΩ
αβγδεζηθικλμνξοπρστυφχψω

on menu) (froóta)
φτάνει *arrives* (ftáni)
φωνάξτε *call, shout*
(fonáxte)

Χ χ
χάθηκα *I'm lost* (háthika)
χαίρετε *hello, or goodbye*
(formal) (hérete)
χαλάσω *(θέλω νά χαλάσω*
. . . I want to change. . .)
(haláso)
χαλάτε *do you*
change . . .? (haláte)
χαρά *(μιά χαρά fine)* (hará)
ο χάρτης *map* (hártis)
ο χασάπης *butcher* (hasápis)
ο χειμώνας *winter* (himónas)
χίλια *one thousand* (hília)
χιλιάδες *thousands*
(hiliádes)
τό χιλιάρικο *thousand-*
drachma note (hiliáriko)
χίλιες *one thousand*
(drachmas) (hílies)
χοιρινή *pork (cutlet)* (hiriní)
τό χοιρινό *pork* (hirinó)
τού χρόνου *next year*
(toó hrónoo)

τό χταποδάκι *octopus*
(htapotháki)
ο χυμός *fruit juice* (himós)
η χωριάτικη *mixed salad*
(horiátiki)
ΧΩΡΙΣ ΕΙΣΠΡΑΚΤΟΡΑ
ONE-MAN OPERATED
BUS (horís ispráktora)

Ψ ψ
τό ψάρι *fish* (psári)
η ψαροταβέρνα *fish*
restaurant (psarotavérna)
η ψησταριά *restaurant*
specialising in grilled
food (psistariá)
ΨΗΤΑ *ROAST DISHES*
(heading on menu)
(psitá)
τό ψωμί *bread* (psomí)

Ω ω
ΩΘΗΣΑΤΕ *PUSH*
(othísate)
η ώρα *hour, time* (óra)
ωραία *fine* (oréa)

εβδομήντα εννιά **79**

Emergency

You can hear how to pronounce these words and phrases at the end of cassette 2, side 2

Be careful	**Προσοχή** Prosohí
Call a doctor	**Φωνάξτε ένα γιατρό** Fonáxte éna yatró
Do you speak English?	**Μιλάτε Αγγλικά;** Miláte Angliká?
Help	**Βοήθεια** Voíthia
I don't understand	**Δέν κατάλαβα** Then katálava
I'm lost	**Χάθηκα** Háthika
I've lost . . .	**Έχασα . . .** 'Ehasa . . .
Look out	**Πρόσεξε** Prósexe
Police	**Αστυνομία** Astinomía

THE Stock Control Card

Customer

HAMMICKS BOOKSHOPS LTD

Account No
780830

ISBN
0340631244

Subject
LANGUAGES

Title
TEACH YOURSELF-HOLIDAY GREEK

Pub Date
06-04-95

Author
GAROUFALIA MIDDLE,H

Supplied Date
22-04-95

Inv. Reference

Inv. No
11364039

*

Qty

Binding
PB

Pub Code Re-order Date
TEAY

Price

Price ex. VAT
4.99

9 780340 631249

Total Home Entertainment
Rosevale Business Park, Newcastle-under-Lyme ST5 7QT
Telephone. Administration 01782 566566 Sales 01782 564455 Returns 01782 566545

THE Re-order Card

Account No
780830

ISBN
0340631244

Title
TEACH YOURSELF-H

Price
4.99

Re-order Qty

Bin ID E10773

Total Home Entertainment
Rosevale Business Park
Newcastle-under-Lyme ST5 7QT
Telephone. Administration 01782 566566
Sales   01782 564455
Returns   01782 566545